Cultivating the Soul
Luigi Zoja

FA^B
Free Association Books

Published in the United Kingdom 2005
by Free Association Books
57 Warren Street
London W1T 5NR
© Free Association Books

All rights reserved, no part of this publication
may be reproduced, stored in a retrieval system,
or transmitted, in any form or by any means,
without the prior permission in writing
of the publisher.

This book is sold subject to the condition
that it shall not, by way of trade or otherwise,
be lent, resold, hired out or otherwise circulated
without the publisher's prior consent in any form
other than that supplied by the publisher.

British Library Cataloguing in Publication Data
A catalogue record for this book is available from the British Library

Produced by Bookchase, London
Printed and bound in the EU

ISBN: 1853437581

Originally published by Moretti & Vitali, Bergamo 1999
Coltivare l'anima / Luigi Zoja
    193 p.
    (Il Tridente Saggi; 5)
    ISBN 88 7186 135 3

CDD. 150.195

Chapters 8 and 17 were translated by Henry Martin, and Chapter 6 was translated by Anthony Molino and Christine Ware. The remaining chapters were translated by John Peck and Mark Kyburz with the assistance of Stefania Zanier.

Wherever a chapter has been printed earlier, the bibliographic information is given at the head of the notes for that chapter.
Gendered third-person pronouns routinely alternate in this translation, with no single convention prevailing.

Editorial Consultant: Anthony Molino

Publisher's note, Moretti and Vitali, 1999

This text is not a book of essays in which an idea is brought forth, developed, and carried to certain conclusions. It is rather like an odyssey—a theme dear to its author—that ventures into unexplored places in our minds, shows corners of habit shunned out of fear or laziness, and withdraws to lonely shorelines, where things loom up suddenly, challenging thought to brave the occasion.

The road that this book travels stretches from the classical world to contemporary society. It is not so much that modernity legislates an interpretation of antiquity; instead the 'modern' psyche frequently gets described from an ancient point of view. The motive for human action is not the passion to learn and to know—as it gripped Oedipus—but the need to live with intensity. Themes such as creation and growth, tragedy and analysis, psyche and society, are all rooted in the symbolic realm and explored in various ways. Thus, even the style changes with the themes: at times we see an artisan at work (patiently exploring etymology or minutely reconstructing historical fact) while at other times a phrase goes in like a shovel, slicing through the inertia of modern thought ('tragedy laughs at our distress') or flows in an almost epic narrative, folding things into its sensory imagery and leading, without our knowing it, to the edge of paradox. As in all true odysseys the goal is not the place to which one comes in the end, but a continuous transformation one undergoes *en route*.

The text includes articles and conference papers written over the course of a decade. Reading them together one witnesses the emergence of a single psychic force: the cultivation of the soul.

To Adolf Guggenbühl-*Craig*

Contents

Preface 13

Part One: *Psyche and Society* 19

Chapter One: 21
    Analytical Psychology and Knowledge of the Other ... 21
Chapter Two 31
    Destructiveness: Tracking its Psychohistory 31
Chapter Three 41
    Truth 41
Chapter Four 49
    James Hillman's Revolution 49

Part Two: *Creation and Growth* 53

Chapter Five 55
    Creation As An Extreme Response to Difficulty 55
Chapter Six 67
    Analysis: Growth or Cure? 67
Chapter Seven 83
    The Need for Growth 83
Chapter Eight 91
    Individuation and Paideía 91
Chapter Nine 125
    Destruction and Creation 125

Part Three: *The Classics Up-To-Date* 131

Chapter Eleven 141
    The Helmet of Hector 141
Chapter Twelve 149
    The Soul of Midas 149
Chapter Thirteen 157
    The Rape of Europa 157

Part Four: *Tragic Thought* 167
Chapter Fourteen.. 169
    The *Agamemnon* and the Contemporary Presence of
        Tragedy 169
Chapter Fifteen 181
    A Different Oedipus 181
Chapter Sixteen 189
    Unhappiness.. 189
Chapter Seventeen 195
    Analysis and Tragedy 195
Chapter Eighteen 221
    In Praise of Not Choosing 221

preface

One day the various forms of psychoanalysis decided that they would no longer shake hands. In fact they did something more baroque and peevish. Since they are always hanging around myths the way dogs hang around bones, they even decided to use myth as a way of breaking up with each other.

They knew very well that their strict denomination was 'depth psychology'. They were thoroughly familiar with the myth of the tower of Babel, at the end of which all go their separate ways because no one can communicate any longer with anyone else.

Therefore they decided to go on living upside-down (it is an ancient and inexorable vocation: they were born to see things all turned around). True psychology does not grow toward the heights but rather the depths. Seeking that and going always deeper, the building of the tower became progressively more difficult and, after a certain point, impossible. Everyone began to speak a different language, and, as a consequence, they formed new families. To deny that the language used by others could serve the articulation of *truth* (strangely enough, this calumny, this falsehood, was true: translated into other tongues, truth no longer uttered 'truth' singularly, but in different ways). In short, they became aware of that which changes, dividing it along particular paths, and lost consciousness of that which remained stable and uniform.

God — or a new god, or a new molecule in their brains that might somehow correspond to some ancient divine plan — confused their languages if not their ideas. In addition, they no longer spoke to each other.

Let us say it right off, so as not to lead the reader astray. This book is born out of that schism. Even if it is a book of Jungian psychology, the rupture it speaks of occurs not between Freud and Jung. It is something else: a differentiation among psychological tendencies that frequently turns up within these same authors. Even within the writings of Freud and Jung.

It is the opposition between that which is stable and general and that which is mute and particular.

The traffic between these two opposing principles does not divide the two founders but actually joins them. In the course of time Freud moved from a strictly clinical interest, in discrete pathologies and single patients, to an interest in mythical and biblical themes about the origin and meaning of civilization. Jung, after a shorter period of psychiatric and experimental work, turned to the study of the archetypes: to religion, anthropology, alchemy, to myths and folktales; to themes that peoples have held in common throughout the most diverse times and places. In short, with the passage of time both masters shifted their attention from pathology — that which diverges from how one might be — to models that speak exactly about how one ought to be.

(In Zurich, *sotto voce* and in suggestive tones of reproach, they still tell the following story. An American arrived in Switzerland to get to know the master, and, after a brief spell, had call to undergo analysis with him. After several sessions, however, Jung looked directly at him and spoke as follows: "I'm sorry, but mostly you talk with me about your parents, and how they shape your dreams. I know that you have got to do this, and I sympathize with you. But I cannot be your analyst; what interest me are the archetypes" (1).)

Through the whole of the twentieth century — and above all during its second half, following the deaths of both masters — the orientation of the principal analytic schools, however troubled, has moved in the opposite direction. Whether among Freud's followers or, in lesser measure yet still appreciably, among those of Jung, there is increasing attention to developmental stages, and therefore precisely to what changes in people as opposed to what is stable in them. In fact, both schools have really concentrated on the earliest phases of life, and therefore, given that society still has little to do at that stage with the young child, they have focused on him as a particular individual rather than as the citizen of a culture or as a being who lives in history.

Nevertheless, one may not conclude that this kind of interest is definitely a preferable one.

It may be prevalent today only because new legislative circumstances are pushing in this direction, both in terms of social class (not to speak of corporations) and of sheer economics. Throughout the world, in fact, the business of psychotherapy has nearly reached a saturation point, and is therefore subject to competition as fierce today as it has been at anytime. This fact, joined to other historical circumstances—for example the rapid growth of European law—has subjected the analytic schools to norms and procedures of institutionalization never seen before. To return to our theme, this movement has shifted the debate between universal and particular. From that which is fixed to that which changes. *From*: what can psychoanalysis, or analytical psychology, say about human beings and about the world? *To*: what can the individual analyst say to the single patient? (And indeed, for just how long and at what rates of invoicing for treatment?) These are the questions that preoccupy bureaucrats and the representatives of the professional psychological classes.

When therefore an analyst has a sufficiently strong voice to still be heard as someone who thinks about human beings in general, rather than some technician in a specific therapeutic school, he can attract an unforeseen number of listeners. James Hillman, for example, enters these pages as the subject of brief reflections on how well he has examined the human condition (for which he has been rightly acknowledged).

The bottom-line is that we are talking about a special case of the swift regression in the political and cultural debate worldwide. With the waning of the ideologies it is no longer a matter of major themes, and we no longer observe real differences between right and left, so that what is involved always seems to be particular and fashionable, and what counts are individual needs. Nevertheless, something of the universal and eternal makes a comeback with all due freshness (Shakespeare in cinema, for example) and meets with an unexpected success (but why unexpected?).

In brief, here is how this book came to be. Some time ago an indefinite sort of request came from an equally indefinable sort of colleague. He is a Greek-Cypriot who has lived in South Africa, taught Jungian psychology in Europe and the East and lives in London. Indeed I shall happily say that he was responsible for the Newsletter sent out to Jungian analysts all over the world. He asked me to send a comprehensive biography and a list of my interests for that publication. I considered that to do any such thing would be like writing one's own obituary, and therefore (if only for good luck) that it was best left to others. However, I also recognized how wrong it was of me to maintain every day that others were mistaken about the point of their lives while putting off the same accounting for myself. With some initial resistance I then began to look into my memory and go through my papers.

After receiving my diploma as an analyst, for a long time I dedicated myself to clinical work and particular problems; for several years, in fact, I returned to Zurich, where I had received my diploma, precisely because the possibility of working in a clinic presented itself there. Nonetheless, my review showed me that over the last decade—which, accidentally or not, was also the last of the century—a growing number of my brief essays and lectures, written for what seem all sorts of reasons, addressed a common need to discover things that change little over the millennia: to know whether certain events that seem contemporary and novel (referring here, for example, to the perverse fascination with television talk shows or with the grief over Princess Diana) are not instead the continuations of myth and its permanence. I allowed myself to be cheered by what I found, for in laying myself bare I discovered that I had taken a road that went towards the greatest and most enduring things, which consequently aimed me, without strain, towards the great masters themselves. In reality this path was not the one I had chosen to take, nor was I aware of it while traveling. Perhaps it is a journey that simply complies with living out one's years, a journey that makes one curious about immortality. Furthermore, one has to realize that what is great and enduring seems to be the image or child of myths.

Myth is one of the few manifestations of immortality that passes before our eyes. We benefit, then, from remembering what the relationship is between the great mythic themes and psychological literature. It was not Sophocles who described the Oedipus complex. And that is so not only because the 'complex' of Oedipus is just one among several possible explanations for its occasion, as well as being unavailable to the eras after Sophocles. It is also because one cannot explain the universal by means of the particular. So if Homer speaks in these pages more than Freud or Jung, one should not think that the pretense of treating loose and general themes of the day has willfully enlisted Homer in this book's service. On the contrary, it is this book—and perhaps the better part of psychological literature—which finds itself becoming a modern and limited voice for what still speaks in Homer and his myths. A link between the two worlds does indeed exist, but it is difficult for depth psychology to do anything to further enrich Homer, who was already far deeper than any psychology.

---

(1) One should add that, with Anglo-Saxon pragmatism, this admirer did not let himself get too discouraged; he went into analysis with Mrs. Jung and in time became one of the world's leading Jungians.

Part One
Psyche and Society

Chapter One

Analytical Psychology and Knowledge of the Other

The expression 'bad teachers' ('*cattivi maestri*') has a wide circulation in Italian, chiefly identifying certain intellectuals who, after having pronounced some revolutionary slogan, found themselves being held morally accountable for the terror and carnage wreaked by the Red Brigades. Abstract language had become concrete destiny, and the word had been made flesh. They could defend themselves only by accusing themselves; they did not have to abide by the letter, or really mean it.

I would like to affirm that quite often these bad teachers have included the foremost Italian masters of the century's greatest, or at least best known, art form: the cinema.

Rosselini's *Roma, Open City*—the film manifesto of neo-realism—portrays average Italians as infinitely pious and generous; with an astonishing lack of criticism we accept the compliment and commit it to memory. De Sica absolves *The Bicycle Thieves*; taking the cue from him, we absolve everyone and make the thief into a national archetype. Fellini tells the story, indulgently and engagingly, of our licentious sexuality and our laziness; we find it delicate and witty, and become exhibitionistic libertines and drifters. We are quite happy that all this wins the approval of Northern Europeans and Americans, and that little meets with their contempt. Perhaps we do not know how to choose our friends, but we certainly understand which friendships are profitable to us.

The point more fundamental to this simplification—a simplification palatable to the masses even though the mass media are still in diapers, and idolized as providing a cinematic renaissance in spite of being kitsch—arrives in a big way with De Santis's *Italiani brava gente* (1964). Ordinary Italians are decent, honest folk (in fact they are fine people, because goodness gets mixed up with idiocy and we have the right to be a little cunning, to retain a bit of the swindler, whilst remaining wholly splendid, indeed among the beautiful people). The Italian character is altogether luminous, nowhere is it shadowy. An Italian has no real enemies; when he deals with allies and enemies he has not done so ambiguously or for commercial advantage, but from his inborn inability to act on hostile impulses.

And so the Italian—and maybe some other lucky people—has no collective shadow.

Shadow, in Jung's psychology, is that part of the unconscious psyche which the first-person singular does not recognize because it is composed of unacceptable moral qualities or, simply, because its otherness is too great. This second meaning, liberally construed, lends greater value to the purposive character of Jungian psychology. Since in Jung's view neurosis is not as an illness but acts as an 'indicator', a momentarily deficient creation, the shadow cannot be seen simply as the inferior, immoral, unacceptable aspect of the personality. That point of view Jung leaves to Freud. According to Jung, the entire psychology of his old master constitutes the greatest study of the shadow that one can imagine (2). In fact, Freud dwelt on the condition still dominated by instinct, which conceals itself below the civilized mind. It bars any return to the archaic, and itself creates nothing new. It stands in irremediable contrast to civilization. Shadow in the ampler Jungian sense is instead the unfamiliar or unexplored factor that contains completeness. It is that in me which I must know if I am to know myself, and that which I must come to know about the world in order to know the real world.

The outcome of all this is quite simple.

Whoever has no shadow is deprived of a fundamental means of knowledge, whether on an individual or collective plane. If I think that I have no shadow (an inferior aspect, either bestial, predatory or simply other than what I usually see), my opposing part and my egoism (archetypes that always belong to the psyche in whatever manner) do not thereby cease to exist. They vanish only as inner qualities, taking up residence in others, outside—as we say, through projection.

The psyche and its archetypes in fact operate not as one single thing—in which case it would already be complete and inoperable—but in complementary dyads. The *Puer* is nothing without its counterpart the *Senex*, youth and old man. On his own the youth does not exist; what we have in fact is a bipolar youth-age archetype. Feminine and masculine do not define themselves in a free-standing way, but as differentials of the opposing sex; and so on. One of these two poles corresponds to the ego, the other remaining inner and unconscious. If I am a man, I carry a woman in my unconscious; I project this inner figure outward and am consumed by a desire to reunite with her. If I am old, nostalgia for youth torments me.

To discover this it is not at all necessary to know Jung. In his *Symposium*, Plato has already narrated these amputations in his own symbolic manner: primordial humanity contained both sexes in a single being, and Zeus therefore split an apparent substantial unity—man and woman—into halves. From then on, tormented by irresistible longing, they try to find each other. In seeking the other we attempt to re-establish original oneness.

Similarly the transference and counter-transference of the analytic relationship are nothing more than expressions of a powerful need to remedy the splitting of an archetypal couple, a wounded figure and a healer, by restoring their union. The therapist, predisposed by vocation, seeks proximity with the patient because he wishes to meet his own shadow full-circle, the wounded one within. The patient, predisposed by illness, wishes to unite with the analyst in order symbolically to recover the healer he carries within, who alone can restore him to stable equilibrium. As long as one's opposite number remains unconscious, it will be projected and perceived only in the other. But this projection is already the beginning of knowledge and a road to the recovery of a certain wholeness.

These facts have often been set forth by Adolf Guggenbühl-Craig (3), who also amplified them with a paradoxical affirmation. Analysts who give in to a temptation to manipulate patients in order to dominate or seduce them will surely be stopped, because the main injury they do is to the value of symbols and only secondarily to professional ethics, the aim of analysis being to bring together not two persons, but rather the two sundered poles of the healer-sufferer archetype.

However, other analysts; those who never fall into similar manipulations because they do not connect with the patient and remain detached, and whose work never manifests erotic tension, are damned in their turn. Not only are they inert, thereby finding it difficult to arouse something in the patient; but they also radiate a cult of self-sufficiency and an indifference to the irreconcilable diversity in our model of the psyche as an organism in constant motion, ever curious, which interminably seeks its own completion. These are the 'beautiful psychotherapists', a disheartening professional subheading of 'beautiful people'.

If we are to stop the first, those who wish to dominate the patient, they—so we hope—will recognize their own mistakes, in which lies concealed a creative hint: the need to know that which is different, and to assimilate it. Therefore, paying the price of error, they will have gotten their ticket for the journey to a more complete life.

The second, however, the self-sufficient analysts, will not be subject to criticism, since those who do not move cannot very well stray from the path. But they will remain strangers on the journey. In the long run they may prove to be more dangerous than the other kind of analyst, because the need to have a confrontation with 'the other half' can hit them with explosive force and find them entirely unprepared.

It is possible to reflect in similar ways on the collective psyche. The ideal would be to live in a society that tolerates differences, conscious and respectful of their existence, whether within its own borders or with respect to neighbouring countries. Since this condition, however, is little more than a fantasy, in reality we find many countries filled with minorities, ethnic diversity, and foreigners, whom the majority seeks to manipulate and put down, alongside a few countries sufficiently homogenous and substantial to furnish a life whose psychology we might call somewhat autistic: it consists in not knowing, indeed in ignoring, the existence of the other.

Among these last, Italy stands in the front rank. With a small Jewish community largely assimilated to Christianity, and traditionally with few immigrants from other continents because it has not remained a colonial power, Italy has not known diversity within its borders. In contrast to other major European languages, English, French, German, Spanish and finally Portuguese, which are all diplomatic or commercial languages, Italian is spoken only in Italy. As for the size of the country, however, its population is sufficiently large to feel no need of learning other languages or of getting to know other nationalities, in contrast, for example, to the Dutch or the Scandinavians who, because of their seafaring traditions, know many other countries quite well, and because of the short reach of their own languages, send their children to work abroad to learn other languages.

Apparently, in the past few centuries, Italy really has not been confronted with diversity either at home or abroad. This deficiency has nourished the commonplace notion of the non-racist Italian, exceptional in a Europe which has invented racism. This notion has bonded, in a vicious circle, with that of the *brava gente*. By means of a falsification that suits everyone, that which was a deficiency turns into a talent.

Therefore, it becomes a genuine national trauma when, within a few years, the influx from developing countries and from Eastern Europe has brought to light in Italy the primitive fellow who distrusts foreigners in the way other countries do but who, unlike those other countries, does not wish to confront them. The police have beaten foreigners because they are foreign; citizens have had recourse to disobedience. They have taken to the streets when faced with the prospect of making room for extending hospitality to refugees who number one tenth, one fiftieth, and at times not even one hundredth the number accommodated by other European countries. These neighbouring countries include of course the formerly racist Germany; and other countries which Italy has prided itself on being different from so that it might go on indulging itself.

When those who suffer arrive, the *brava gente* shut their doors. It is deemed to be normal and normally wicked, but exists without any habitual wrestling with the shadow, principally because the splendid member of this class has never lived out the history of this confrontation nor of its atonement, which can be mapped from events like the Nuremberg Trials or South Africa's Commission for National Reconciliation. Essentially, between the Nazi extermination camps and a Somalian burnt alive in a Roman street there exists an enormous quantitative difference, but no qualitative one. From our viewpoint a crime against humanity is equal to a crime against the psyche, because the response it brings to the psyche's natural interest in diversity seeks not to comprehend it, but to destroy it. Rejecting everything originating outside ourselves, we quash any possibility of knowing the other within ourselves.

Like the inner world, our geographic world is composed of stitching and fractures, unions and sunderings. Today sees the healing of that wound which, designated as an 'Iron Curtain' in 1946, had divided Europe 'from Stettin to Trieste'.

We had thought this would forever remain as the emblem of global division and of the irreconcilable other. How naïve we were: some twenty years of ideological rivalry leaves no deep mark, blowing as mere spindrift across the ocean of history.

The world's fault line, however, has not vanished. On the contrary, it separates East and West, North and South. Which is to say that this breach is scored twice over, because the present hour, regardless of the side from which one sees it, divides lesser from greater with an enormous symbolic weight. Above all because it repeats the millennarian experience, trawling the depths of the past. Its scar tissue separates not only North and South, but also Europe (significantly, carried off amorously by the king of the gods himself) and Africa (which for Europeans in antiquity meant only Carthage, and which, due to Rome's hostility to Carthage as 'the other', as a whole came to mean 'the dark continent'). It separates whites from blacks (their shadow), and Indo-Europeans from Semites. Whoever thinks that anti-Semitism—the systematic negation of the other on ethnic grounds—is a creature of our time need only peruse a volume of history to see the scrupulous care with which Rome annihilated Jerusalem and Carthage.

This fissure therefore cuts across the collective unconscious of the Italian peninsula. Even in border regions a fusion has come about. On the western tip of Sicily the remains of Greek and Phoenician cities overlap each other. Within such a mixture, however, one immediately discovers a large difference among the images that have been left behind. The sculpture of the Indo-Europeans (the Greeks) insisted upon the human figure, while conversely that of the Semites (Phoenician and Carthaginian) sends it packing. Over the millennia, this radical difference is the same distinction which even today separates religious art among Christians from that of Muslims and Jews.

The aforementioned unconscious factor sinks into the depths of history, and with it goes every violent opposition.

Whoever denies this factor does not side with goodness, but instead with a quite literal egoism, since he denies existence to 'the other'. The projection of shadow constitutes a particularly dangerous moment of unconsciousness which must be analyzed, a moment which at the same time is critically important. If this happens, if it catches itself for inspection, if it does not immediately seek to annihilate the shadow-other because it dreads that part of ourselves which it symbolically represents, the encounter is also the first phase in the consciousness of these same things, and the escape from the dangerous illusion of being a splendid or beautiful person. The conviction that one has no enemies is not, in fact, a stage that follows the projection of the shadow-other. In many respects it is, on the contrary, an antecedent condition, still more unconscious, in which the I—or the We—finds it difficult to stand distinct and apart from the You.

Jung devoted several pages of his *Memories, Dreams, Reflections* to his encounter with North Africa. At the end of his journey in Tunisia, he refers to having had a long dream in which he was confronted by a noble Arab. In the dream he succeeded in getting the better of his opponent after a long struggle. He held back from killing him. At the end, he obliged the Arab to collaborate by reading to him a text written in an oriental tongue, which Jung could not decipher alone although he sensed that it was meant for him (it was, Jung says, 'my book'; it had been written for him) (4).

The encounter of the European with the Arab is the encounter with the other. Referring again to the dream, it becomes the collision with the shadow. This clash with the shadow becomes an encounter with a fundamental part, and apparently an exclusively hostile part, of the Self: it becomes consciousness. The Jung who struggles in the dream with his Arab opponent is like Jacob who, in the Biblical episode (*Genesis* 32: 25-33), wrestles with the angel.

That struggle takes place in the dark—in the dream for Jung, at night for Jacob—which is to say in the unconscious. The challenge is to avoid being killed by one's adversary, and also to refrain from killing him, as long as the darkness lasts. When light returns, then the meaning which the struggle bore will become determinate, the standoff will fall away, and the enemy will reveal himself to be a divine support: an angel of the Most High. If we are believers, let us not pray that the struggle with our neuroses and the conflicts with our adversaries in the world go away. Let us pray that they go on, but as steps on the ascent to consciousness.

Paper delivered in French at the conference on *Mahgreb at the Cultural Crossroads*, in the portion devoted to *Jung and Africa* (Hammamet, Tunisia, 1997) and printed in the conference papers.

(2) C. G. Jung, *Collected Works* 10, para 353; 11, para 351, 941; 16, para 145, 173, etc.
(3) Adolf Guggenbühl-Craig, *Power in the Helping Professions*. Spring, New York, 1971.
(4) *Memories, Dreams, Reflections*, tr. Richard and Clara Winston. Pantheon, New York, 1963, Chapter IX, pp. 242-244.

Chapter Two

Destructiveness: Tracking its Psychohistory

The figure of the hero is among the least volatile of models in the hyper-volatile history of the West. In spite of millennia, the custom amongst us still exists that the Greek heroes are always the supreme ideal. Among them Odysseus is the most complex, the most complete, the most modern.

Yet we in the West have lost awareness of our traditions of aggression, believing that we have banished hatred, violence and war from our values, and so we no longer know what we are doing when we ask our children to study the *Odyssey*.

In Book XIX, the old nurse Eurycleia washes the feet of a beggar, a guest at the palace of Odysseus and Penelope, whom the reader already knows to be Odysseus in disguise. When Eurycleia recognizes the hero through an old scar, Homer suspends the action to recount the origin of that wound. Yet, as is usually the case, he tells a thoroughly complicated story. From here we learn that Odysseus has inherited the temperament of his maternal grandfather, Autolycus, 'a great thief and swindler'. But that is not all that he received from him. Autolycus, through a play on words, had also given his own name to his grandson: "I have come here as one called *odyssámenos* [which means filled with hatred and fury]: therefore let him be called *Odisseo*" (XIX.407-9). From the same root *od-*, according to authoritative etymologists, comes the Latin *odium* and every modern expression that indicates hatred.

Therefore, the name Odysseus signifies 'he who hates'.

Yet even so, without turning to linguists (for whom words preserve traces of original meaning which the mind has forgotten) the children in our schools are on familiar terms with such anger. They have read the *Odyssey*, and know that its protagonist is pumped up with wrath. Shortly afterwards, in fact, the bow of Odysseus will exterminate the Suitors one by one, in spite of their offer to surrender and pay ample reparations. After the massacre, an even worse fate will come to the serving women and the goatherd Melanthios, who had served the Suitors.

This is the model of classical heroism that we still hold up to our children. Yet, contradictorily, we reject the aggressive quality in Odysseus as hero. It remains far removed from those values that we claim inspire us. Let us reflect: would anyone today call his own son 'he who hates'?

If the prototypical epics come from Homer, our primary moral models are from the Old Testament and speak much the same language. In the second discourse of *Deuteronomy*, the Mosaic code, we find the rules of war. When taking a foreign city, 'You shall put all its males to the sword', it suggests (XX.13); but if it be a neighbouring town which the Lord has given to you, 'you shall save alive nothing that breathes' (XX.16).

The people under Joshua show a similar zeal on the taking of Jericho: 'they utterly destroyed all in the city, both men and women, young and old, oxen, sheep, and asses, with the edge of the sword' (Joshua 6.21).

Just as aggressive, as is well-known, are the mythology and religion of the Germanic peoples, which in north-central Europe form the substrate onto which the Greco-Roman and Christian layers grafted themselves. It will suffice to touch on Wotan, the chief god, who is the god of battle. His name, no different than Odysseus, derives from *Wut* or fury.

Then, too, if we go back behind historical humanity to prehistoric humankind, paleontology and ethnology show us that the human species stands as an exception among the surviving kinds because it murdered its species kin (5): that is, it is similar from the viewpoint of zoology and its fellow men from the Christian viewpoint. Working back toward our origins, with finds from the Neolithic, Mesolithic and Paleolithic, one continually comes up against skulls smashed in by stone axes. We implore the objects found in these excavations to tell us how far back in time one must go to encounter the lost paradise of Rousseau. Yet no answer comes. Whether it be in myth, or in rock engravings more ancient than any myth, they show humans striking down their own kind.

Metamorphosis

In antiquity, the whole temperament of the person had dignity, not only the good portion exclusively. This totality included the demonic complexes, particularly the ones endowed with power, from which a man, more than a woman allows himself to possess his features of character. This total man, from whom the destructive passions are not separable, has received his statutory aesthetic from the moderns who have dubbed his qualities as 'the tragic world'. Hölderlin, Nietzsche, and Burckhardt have viewed from this position the highest point of any civilization. He is the total subject because he totally takes on (humbly, we may say, so long as the word does not sound Christian) his own two-faced nature, creative and destructive at the same time. 'I know what my acts have in store for me, but my will is trampled by fury, the cause of mankind's greatest evils' (*Medea*, 1078-80).

The depth of reflections on evil produced by the tragic mind tilled the ground for the sowing and rapid flowering of Christianity in the following centuries. The mask of tragedy, on which an already inscribed demonic evil had modeled itself, was thereafter relegated to archaeology. Christianity gained the upper hand by establishing the supremacy of good over evil, rather than globally incorporating evil, and has erected stable categories of good and evil that were at last clear and distinct, refuting that destiny which consigned humanity to ambivalence. This distinction without compromise was not an utter novelty on the part of Christianity. It had already been thoroughly elaborated by Judaism and then carried forward in debates among the philosophers, especially Plato. But it became truth for the elites, or the intellectuals, only when Christianity became truth for every social class and did so throughout the West.

As for the tragic man, who knows and accepts his own destructiveness, he surrendered his place to the ideal of the good man. The total man yielded to the man of distinct categories, and destiny to free will.

To square accounts, we need to bring into focus what constitutes an evolution for morality and then address another issue.

The interesting point here in fact involves several things at once. Just as in a theatre, where the more the spotlights focus on the stage, the more the rest of the space grows indistinct, so too, in distinction from the tragic man who blended into the shadows, the kind of person reborn from the Christian revolution, and then the Enlightenment, and then the scientific revolution, thereby always choosing more precisely and one-pointedly what was good, he tries therefore to make himself one with goodness as much as possible.

The first risk in this evolution is aesthetic attrition. Consider the complexity of an archaic poem like the *Iliad*. The Trojans are no different than the Greeks, like them in being complex human creations, compounded of good and evil. Therefore, Homer's favourite hero is the Trojan Hector.

Likewise the first Greek historian, Herodotus, was called *philobarbaros* because he placed his own people and the barbarians on the same level. Aeschylus in turn, describing the Persian Wars in one of his plays (namely *The Persians*), considered it more important to stage the tribulations of defeated barbarians than the triumph of the Greeks. Next to Homer's poem or the tragedies of Aeschylus, a masterpiece of Christian epic like *The Song of Roland* seems surprisingly shallow; its Saracens are a horde of brats, while the Christian paladins are boring fashion plates who gleam with unshadowed radiance.

The graver risk, however, is that of psychic loss, an excess of simplification deriving from the elimination of evil. Gradually the aggressive, shadowy, and chthonic forms of the divine are banished from history and relegated to folklore. The destructive and demonic element, which no culture ever manages to cancel out as a psychic possibility (and therefore, sooner or later, as a practical outcome: witness as proof the tragic consequences of the Marxist utopia), stays across from the main stage, in the darkness. It is always known with greater difficulty, and always more easily denied, than a symbol in plain sight.

As every depth psychology teaches, we condemn our own most fearful qualities. Yet while the most destructive instincts may be denied, they may not be eliminated; they are perceived in others as wickedness. Suspicion, malevolence, and irrational hatred are the final links in a destructive chain forged out of withdrawal, negation, splitting, and projection of these qualities onto adversaries. The relentless progress of the West has taught us ever increasingly to think in clear and positive categories. In behaving this way, the Western world has marginalized those categories which are dark and negative, and has obscured that complex and chiaroscuro-like vision which lets us look out through the eyes of others.

With the Greeks, the enemy is, yes, killed, but only with difficulty is he hated with persecutory rage, because the demonic complex is not habitually split off from the subject and projected onto the opponent. The standardization of clear-cut conceptions of good and evil goes along with the creation of the psychological conditions behind the Crusades, the Inquisition, the genocide of the Indians, the World Wars, the *Shoah* and the Iron Curtain.

An ordinary person experiences evil through the intervening persona rather than knowing it and overcoming it. Such conquest is reserved for the saint, who nonetheless does not eradicate destructiveness, but recognizes it in himself as the dark side produced by the lights of sanctity and the law; or, from another point of view, as the internal face of the tragic mask. Paul perceives this sharply once more when he says, 'I do not understand my own actions. For I do not do what I want, but I do the very thing I hate' (*Romans* 7.15), and again, 'For I do not do the good I want, but the evil I do not want is what I do' (*ibid*. 7.19).

The Present

The moral evolution of the West corresponds, from the viewpoint of manifest values, to a disappearance of demonic symbols.

In the history of the psyche this resembles a gradual sanitizing of the upper storey, which deposits the germs, along with the darkness of the personality, in the storey below: in this cellarage the microbes also go on growing so long as no one is looking. Alongside strictly historical, political and social factors, precisely this psychic infection is co-responsible for the generalized destructiveness of the First World War. Thereafter, Europe was laid out on the worktable of a tailor-executioner who, to put a modern face on it, tortured Europe with nationalistic scissors and stitch-work. From this 'revolution of limits' has come an inexhaustible series of other wars. Since even today we pay the price for this with new, explosive nationalisms, we may suspect, too, that the executioner is not free from the demonic impulse that had animated the same war.

European war in the twentieth century implies a new kind of psychology. For the first time in history, conquered peoples take on the condition of the guilty rather than the defeated. What is not taken into account is that while war reparations may be more or less supportable, extending a supporting hand only to those who apply, the assignment of enormous guilt is a profound and revolutionary event for the psyche, which requires the conversion of the subject to this interpretation, or, as it happens, a paranoid rejection. In this way the first postwar period activated the demonic complex rather more than did the war itself, leading without interruption to the Second World War.

Since I have mentioned the flight of Wotan, it may be worth pointing out that the rebirth of German militarism and the swift acclamation of National Socialism have been interpreted, aside from a redemption of such guilt, precisely as the return of the ancient Germanic god of war, from whom the Brown Shirts adopted more than a few of their rituals. Hitlerism was also the return of destructive paganism in the people, which was more available to them because they had been Christianized relatively late. In this sense, the war corresponded to an unconscious reissue of *Ragnarök*, the final battle in which all the Germanic gods must perish.

Not usually placed in high relief, this particular aspect is all but unique to the Germanic gods. No sooner do they make their appearance than they relinquish immortality, and their mythology is constantly fraught with the consciousness of death. So the cult of the god of war is not only the cult of destructive aggression turned outward against others. It was the expectation of total destruction, including one's own. In Hitlerism the identification with Wotan corresponded to the consciousness that battle would have carried death to all parties—not only to them but also to us. Consistent with this collectivist passion on the part of Wotan—vowed to the enemy's demise but also to one's own—the military campaigns with which Hitler celebrated the god's cult on the battlefield would arrive directly with growing irrationality against mounting adversaries: an apocalypse where every life—the protagonist or the enemy, good or bad—is destroyed. In Hitler's case, in contrast to that of normal commanders, he scheduled and elaborated plans not only for conquest but also the meticulous *Nerobefehl* (the Nero Order, March 1945) (6) which stipulated an obliteration of structures still vital to Germany: utterly foreign to the motives of regular strategy, and understandable only as possession by a destroying god. The demise of the last Germanic gods, so convincing in itself, was the final act which eliminated demonic symbolic forms from the realm of conscious values. With this final arrangement of his, the Führer finally revealed that he had not waged war for the benefit of the German people, but for those ancient gods and for the enactment of their tragic destiny ending in death.

In the second postwar period the concepts used by many political bodies superficially cleansed themselves of aggressive meanings: Departments of War became Departments of Defense, and espionage agencies turned into counter-espionage. Yet aggression, as a psychological and cultural quality, not only failed to disappear but in fact so much became the case in Europe that life organized itself around the Cold War and the Iron Curtain. Demonization of the adversary was to be structured from the individual level right up to that of the mass media.

In a few years this enormous paranoia, dragging its knife across nations and single minds alike, crumbled away. But in this manner, at one stroke, we find ourselves with our devils once again on our own hands, lacking the convenient enemy in whose reliable care we may leave them. We are used to identifying with the good and canceling out our destructive impulses, which we assign to adversaries. The Western tradition, in contrast to Hinduism, for example, by this time has suppressed the destructive forms of its own conscious symbols. This habit is very old, and therefore difficult to change quickly. However, when once upon a time we have eliminated the enemy and his atomic weapons, we must also realize that destructiveness will still exist and reside, as a potential impulse, in each one of us. In this light the fall of the Iron Curtain is not only as it is usually thought to be, a momentous political event, but also an occasion for unprecedented psychic maturation.

If we limit ourselves to smothering the same things in ourselves and expelling from official culture the demonic forms that still have life, we can expect that they will turn up more and more in the pathological forms already diffused throughout the West, or rather show up on the lowest level, as a pseudo or subculture that officially gets turned into a wild football match or brand of music, but in reality is devoted to the cult of the ancient god of aggression.

The propriety of our values has generated its own opposite: young people who, turning once more to the culture of the *Odyssey*, could refer to themselves as 'the people who hate'.

As delivered at the FIP Conference (Federation of Italian Psychologists) on *Violent Thinking*, in Rome, 1991.

(5) I. Eibl-Eibesfeldt, *Etologia della Guerra* (1979). Borighieri, Torino, 1990.
(6) R.D. Müller and Uegberschâr, *La fine del terzo Reich* (1994). Il Mulino, Bologna, 1995.

Chapter Three

Truth

Before using an important term like *truth*, we ought to clarify what we are talking about. Everyone, especially psychologists, somberly makes a long face at this word. We leave unspoken the fact that truth deals with the ultimate quality that justifies any thought or action without requiring any justification in turn.

To keep faith with the specificity of psychology, one must distinguish between the truth of the psyche and the external form of truth to which it stands opposed.

The first corresponds to everything that acts upon inner life. That which moves me inwardly, touches me, raises emotion or works on me independently of my intention, is psychologically true, or constitutes psychic reality (Jung called it the reality of the anima). This meaning of truth has no bearing on making an objective verification (*verum-facere*). On the contrary, in a certain sense it comes down to belief, although quite far from an institutional faith. It has to do with what makes sense to me, with how much it meets with my trust (*fiducia*: from *fides*) and becomes an object of my belief, all such processes answering neither to reason nor will. *True* in the psychological sense is something quite independent of logical procedure and remote from conscious intention (and therefore also from material verification, because one may not set it in relation to the idea of a starting point): a religious faith, an artistic inspiration, the state of being in love or even in a psychotic delirium. To devalue such ultimacy with the etiquette of 'false' constitutes a dangerous dismissal of psychic reality, which always has importance whether individual or social. In the individual, we must at least grant it the respect of an affliction that sees its own meaning; in the social realm, we must at least take account of the negative ravings that call out for the annihilation of dangerous enemies and have real and drastic consequences—in fact, if the enthusiast gains access to political power, even catastrophic ones.

The second or external truth is a secular quality that regulates the daily things of the world: an attribute which we recognize as being present in them and thereby worthy of our respect, but irrelevant to our interiority.

This quality is foreign to trust and does not produce the sense of life. However much science and knowledge continually add to it, this truth will never suffice, nor ever make up for want of the other kind. For example, truth in this sense is a theorem in geometry; it is said that no one has ever been killed by a geometrical theorem, while all the time millions die happily for a crazy idea which for them, however, is endowed with meaning.

It is undeniably the case that we always need some truth of the first kind, while it seems that we can quietly do with less of the other. Not that it ceases running our circumstances, but it can operate without our knowing it and leave us indifferent.

The first truth, the psychic kind, comes to us—we choose neither when nor how it does so—with a force greater than our own: it holds the rank of a religious value. Only the second kind lets us approach it as we please. The first truth finds in the psyche that organ through which it manifests itself, while the second expresses itself in the universal organ of nature.

Only the second truth, this lower, ordinary, non-psychic kind, can be rationally administered. Day after day, the bookkeeper builds an accountancy for the firm that can be called true without fail. At the end of the week, therefore, he can leave, quite removed from this truth which corresponds only to what it contains; and then on Monday he builds it from scratch again. This same book-keeper, therefore, cannot adhere with conviction to a determined faith—feeling it as if it were his own inner truth—during certain days of the week and alienate himself on others; nor, we might suppose, may he decide to be in love on Wednesday and not Thursday.

The two meanings of truth correspond to two meanings of law: inner law and natural law. If we ignore the first type of law we shall feel at odds with ourselves, and this is so quite aside from the fact that it replaces a correct or failed morality. The norm that governs our life as commandment has a global function: to aim at and provide equilibrium not only to society but also to our minds, our psychology. We need not occupy ourselves, on the other hand, with natural law, whose self-respecting operations have no need of interventions from us. The laws of physics, chemistry and so on (and the truth these branches of science contain) govern human life without calling on us to become culpable and to learn about them, having governed animal life or inorganic matter prior to human existence.

Fundamentally we have said a very simple thing. Some truths 'have to be' as the sun has to rise: they predate our discovery and enter the brain but not the soul. Other truths instead have to be seen as integral to our duty. It is our task constantly to construct them: they spring up as autonomous impulses of the soul, and from there prevail over the mind and eventually our behaviour. They may correspond to a collective exigency—a faith—or an individual one—falling in love; but they have in common the fact that there is no gainsaying them.

It has been shown (7) that antiquity recognized two thoroughly distinct kinds of truth. Greek truth is cognitive and, for its time, secular; it refers to something which already exists in some manner and which becomes perceptible to the subject when it succeeds in overcoming the obstacles which conceal it: it is a revelation, *a-letheia*, an emergence from a hidden condition. Hebraic or monotheistic truth is instead a commandment, a moral quality of the subject itself, which one meets with again more in the modern notions of coherence, firmness and so on, than in specific stipulations. Yet it must be noted that, through the transformations and universalization of Judiasm in Christianity, the idea of truth which has given shape to the history in which we still live today is religious and directive. Even now, to hear the word *truth* makes it easier to raise one's voice or lay hold of a knife.

This is the moment to underscore one of the most profound paradoxes of our modernity. Within the context of modernity, science has prevailed over religion as an unquestioned and prevalent form of truth. But this disenchanted, rational world, which unilaterally identifies its own good with the effects of uninterrupted progress, puts into practice beneath its own secular garb the deeply monotheistic attitude of Christianity and, more inwardly, of Judaism. The motive advanced by dominant techno-scientific truth is not external, resting nowhere in the autonomy of natural law which automatically discloses itself. Instead, such truth is a commandment mounting the stairway that climbs into the heaven of progress and advertises itself through its limitless output. Taken by itself, nothing in all this is very important; while the criterion of truth, however, is a substantial act of faith, singular and never disavowed, which believes in progress and enforces it, a measure of the perpetual and specifically European Christian will to transform each good thing into something better. It matters little if hopes have been secularized and what is good wears the expression of mere things. So it is that the religious extends any heroic leap, through which progress proliferates its offspring, its technological adherents, precisely as the faithful must increase, multiplying themselves and showing forth in everyone's good works. Likewise, truth is a greater body of rational knowledge, a growth in experience, a greater number of personal relationships or trips abroad, of personal possessions, *ad infinitum*.

The paradox of the open world, created by European culture in the modern era, is that it has generalized secularism and a definitive form of toleration but derives its momentum from the religious and biblical roots of truth. As one of Camus's characters puts it, truth today is still a command (8). This world professes that it is *en route* to pluralism, but the engine to which it has entrusted itself is totalitarian.

The world that is categorically open and irreversibly modern sets out with the voyage of Columbus. That very year, however, is the one in which the same Spanish king promulgates the Edict of Grenada, with the expulsion and expropriation of hundreds of thousands of Jews. Christian Europe already retained possession of the one and only truth but, due to the flaws of its technical and administrative tentacles, it also continually played host to unclassifiable affairs of cultural and religious diversity. Paradoxically, just as 1492 assumed the mantle of modern history's inception, it also inaugurated an intolerant totalitarian application of the idea of truth, which extends down through to Auschwitz, but has yet to reach its end.

We regard totalitarianism as a decadent and terminal form of belief. But from the viewpoint of psychodynamics the lineages of totalitarianism are irrelevant. They can take up space in the vast depths of the psyche the way water fills a vessel: the psyche is a natural process, which responds to the constellations of a commandment-like truth as the paradoxical root of the modern secular world. Marxism had replaced a Christianity grown stiff and moribund, much as totalitarianism was probably the stagnantly impounded phase of an already decaying Marxism. One of the tools with which Marxism initiated planetary suicide was precisely its thesis that it was a scientific truth, which rendered it vulnerable to any contradiction or failure. It would have been different if, more consistently with itself, it had been proclaimed as a creed, a metaphysical path of salvation.

As for ourselves, a not dissimilar risk weighs upon psychoanalysis. It studies the laws that govern the psyche, but everything depends on clarifying what is meant by law. Not laws in the sense of rules that describe the geography of the psyche as geometry describes the rules by which planar figures or solids are generated, but laws in the sense of inner imperatives. Not definite and stable natural laws, but forms that carry passion and have meaning, laws ever-changing with the times, culture and individual temperament.

Psychic truth is something that can be neither programmed nor objectively verified. With such truth it is clear from the outset that one agrees to work with things through conflict and irrationality, which would appear, in the case of a fixed meaning as borrowed from the natural sciences, to be out of the picture. If a communal, fixed and defining standard of what constitutes psychic truth were to be determined in advance, the incompatibility would be even greater and more defining; in fact this would seem to be impossible. An attempt to attain it would resemble a religious war. Paradoxically, the archaic and fideistic criterion of psychic truth as an inner religion is a preventative that can protect against external religious conflicts and their totalitarianisms.

We shall no longer be able to compose irrefutable manuals of psychology like those for the natural sciences. Will we be able to regard them without envy?

We westerners fear that the domination of objective truth by a truth of faith represents a setback or regression. But such is not always the case, depending on the context. In a society based on belief, for example those we call primitive, magical truth can outclass objective verity as being more effective and more true.

Let us reflect on a case from the Kwakiutl reported by Franz Boas (9). Quesalid wanted to apprentice himself to a shaman, not in order to undergo genuine initiation but to learn the tricks that shamans use and to unmask their pretentious charlatanism. Before approaching a sick person, they place an object in their mouths, and then, having performed ceremonies and recited hysterical routines, they round off the cure by spitting out the object which should constitute, in the sufferer's reckoning, the illness driven out by the shaman. Quesalid carried through with what was expected of him, anticipating the advent of his secular truth. It did not arrive, however. For when Quesalid had performed his trick through to its finale, the afflicted man was cured. What on earth? Traditionally, psychic irrational truth has taken effect through the rapport between patient and healer, even if the latter was persuaded that it was hopelessly old-fashioned and therefore thought it useless in a healer's hands.

In a rather similar manner we dedicate ourselves to modern psychotherapy. At first we come like initiates to the truths of Freud or Jung as to an incontrovertible belief. Then, after years of practice, we imperceptibly lose the passion, the élan, not to say the conviction that the foundational principles with which we work are always beneficial and precise. Sooner or later, like the Church which gradually rose from the secrecy of the catacombs to the halls of temporal power, we leave a fading psychic truth and barter it for a detached secular outlook. Our patients, however, go on getting better, and in extreme cases do so even if we no longer believe in the idea that we claim to be applying. Psychic truth is evidently a principle strong enough to prevail against even the neglect of personal duty.

---

(7) S. Quinzio, *La croce e il nulla*. Adelphi, Milano, 1984.
(8) Albert Camus, *La peste* [*The Plague*]. Gallimard, Paris, 1947.
(9) This is taken from an ancient Kwakiutl text related in full in Claude Levi-Strauss, *Structural Anthropology*, Chapter IX, 'The Sorcerer and His Magic'. London, Allen Lane/Penguin, 1958, pp. 167ff. (The same material also appears in Henri Ellenberger, *The Discovery of the Unconscious: The History and Evolution of Dynamic Psychiatry*. New York, Basic Books, 1970, pp. 10-12.)

Chapter Four

James Hillman's Revolution

The man who observes puts his point of view at the center of the scene which he observes: such is the price one pays for being a person rather than an impersonal perceptual apparatus. Croce refers to this point when he says that every history is a contemporary history, and Toynbee elaborates on it when he states that to write history is to do battle with egocentricity.

James Hillman speaks of this with respect to the maladies of civilization. Because he extracts a moral essence from these, we may fairly enroll him in that chain of innovators who have done battle with the egocentrism that we rely on in dealing with the circumstantial world, and who have had to teach us humility. This chain has been assembled by Freud, who in fact spoke of the *humiliation* inflicted on human narcissism by new knowledge, and set down its name alongside that of pride at our arrival gate (10).

According to Freud, the first assault on egocentrism was the blow delivered to geocentrism by astronomy. Until then the *Earth*—with capital letter, the name of our planet—uncritically corresponded in various languages to *earth*—the lower-case ground under our feet, because it was thought to be the only possible point of view. Just as many primitive tribes give themselves a name whose contemporary sense is 'The Humans', whose subtext is that no other people exists, and no other peoples exist beyond ours, and no other earth exists beyond the Earth. With the Copernican revolution the Earth ceased to be the center of the universe, having been changed into one of an infinite and rather insignificant number of points.

Then anthropocentrism received a blow. In zoology, humanity had occupied the position of the sun in our solar system. With the Darwinian revolution it ceased being the fixed center of life forms, becoming only one link in an infinite chain undergoing infinite mutation. A certain inferiority came from this straightaway, turning humanity into the monkey's cousin.

Then it was modern psychology's turn to assault egocentrism on its home ground. With Freud the ego, that part of psychic activity which appears to constitute everything and which corresponds to both will and consciousness, finally squeezes itself into being merely the tiny, visible tip of an iceberg which makes up the internal psychic apparatus. The invisible mass of it—dreams, fantasies, and irrational impulses—was always part of our psyche, but unconscious. The ego lost not only its central position in the outer world, but in the inner realm as well.

Freud, however, like Moses with whom he later identified himself, had managed to get to the Promised Land without entering it. A kind of imperialism of the ego still resounded in his exhortation, 'Where Id is Ego shall be'. It was Jung who completed the Exodus. The unconscious is made up not only of forgotten and repressed contents; it contains the genetic code of the psyche, and exists prior to the ego, which derives from it and not vice versa. Directly one sees that it is common to everyone and contains a universal language, to which myths testify. Its submerged portion is a single, boundless mass, in which the whole of humankind comes together with the pre-conscious animal realm. The ego shrivels once more, the encounter this time making it infinitely small.

Among these ruins, in the vale of the illusions and certainties of omnipotent egocentrism, we encounter James Hillman. With a single radical gesture, Hillman knocks down the anthropocentric soul. In Italian, 'anima' is a stand-in for the psyche, a category of religious debate. For Hillman, who has turned back to Neo-Platonic and Renaissance traditions, *soul* or anima is a quality—though it would be better to say a reality—perceived psychically but not necessarily a quality of the psyche itself. In essence, it comes down to something quite simple: to return to the superior understanding of the young child, the primitive, or the East not yet distorted by a pervasive European narcissism. It does not require much effort to recognize a similarity between animals, a soul in things, and in all of them a swarm of gods: to accept Darwin then is to accept Hillman now.

The psyche may be seen as an organ that alerts and plays host to the soul, but is not identical with it: a distinction similar to the Hillmanian one between civilization (stable) and culture (which bursts in upon and nourishes civilization) (11). With Hillman, therefore, as already in the ancient idea of the *anima mundi* or world soul, the soul is anything but something internal and subjective, and not simply because, as psychology traditionally says, it gets projected or put out on loan to the outer world by human subjects. The soul of the environment exists even though we do not perceive it. In fact, our own miniscule soul is in large part the product of that environment, and not only of the natural one.

Hillman addresses architects and urban planners—at their congresses, for example—and not in order to propose some ingenuous restoration along naturalistic lines. Human beings give form to the urban environment, but at the same time are formed by it. Desiccation in the souls of buildings produces husks of citizens. The hollow and squared-off forms of fascism and socialist realism create emptied-out and confrontational human beings. Whoever denies this is perhaps afraid that their spiritual qualities will revert to stone or cement, as Darwin's opponents were afraid of descending from monkeys. Hillman has invited psychoanalysts (12) to look at the outer world, applying treatment to the narcissism of their discipline, which is more subjective than that of their patients. Since then he has turned his attention to the soul that surrounds us, even going as far as the business environment in his most recent book (13).

Humility is a necessary food for the life that is lived at peace with itself. Holy Writ stipulated humility as a moral commandment, but also recommended the pride that goes with being at the center of existence, creatures of a god who plays favourites. Breaking down egocentrism, the great revolutions should have made over to us a reasonably humble equanimity. Dismantling the Bible, they have instead granted us reason stripped of either peace of mind or humility. If the price of consciousness is the loss of both glory and story, it is hard to restore consciousness to greater morality and humility: made anxious by virtue of falling outside a grand narrative, narcissists try to turn back to the centre, only to find themselves consigned in short order to the seven sins or to psychotherapy.

It is impossible for us to know where Hillman's 'revolution' is going. We do know, however, that it could teach respect for a soul that is far more than one's personal possession, and could include it in a plot wherein, unlike the story that psychoanalysis writes in order to produce knowledge, it is impossible to explain anything without also telling a story. Its gaze conveys consciousness without being disenchanted; and its gods have abandoned the heavens, the seas and the springs, not in order to vanish, but to hide out in the computer.

First published as an article in *Il Sole 24 Ore*, 26 June 1996.

(10) Sigmund Freud, *The Difficulty of Psychoanalysis* (1916). In *Works*, Standard Edition, vol. VIII.
(11) *Aut Aut* 264, November-December 1994.
(12) *Dal narcissismo alla finestra*, in P. Aite and A. Carotenuto, *Itinerari del pensiero junghiano*. Cortina, Milano, 1989.
(13) James Hillman, *Kinds of Power*. Currency, New York, 1995.

Part Two
Creation and Growth

Chapter Five

Creation As An Extreme Response to Difficulty

Two thousand years of Christianity have predisposed us to think very little about creation as a human event, consigning it to the domain of absolute ideas: the creator *par excellence* is the one who makes things leap up out of nothing.

This way of putting it has made the fact of creation largely incomprehensible, relegating it to a heap of things taken on faith. Bringing the idea of creation back to the suffering and cramped arena of human action is a matter, then, of digging into and rediscovering its original meaning.

Creo in Latin means to produce, to (make) grow. In fact *cresco* (in Italian *crescere*) is precisely the root term from which *creo* stems and branches out, finally forming the transitive expression 'I grow" (cresco), while saying "creo" indicates a growth instigated by something other than me. Latterly, in the Christian era, the idea of creation submitted to a shift in meaning, and signified a theological connotation. With a slide that corresponds to the Latin expression, the Greek New Testament also changes the usage of the verb *ktízo*. A similar shift shows up in a later period in German. Today the verb *schöpfen* means creation from nothing, but its root shares common ground with *schaffen*, which has the rather more general sense of producing, generating and making, and which in turn has an ancient source linked to *schaben* (Latin *scabo*), the act of rasping or scraping, which expresses one of the earliest and most generalized forms of working with a tool.

Creation as a superior and divine prerogative is therefore present in European languages not as an original meaning, but as a 'theological deformation', stamped into place by Christian thought in its progressive elaboration of categories for the supernatural.

Monotheism differentiated itself from polytheism through the presence of a creator god no less than through its unification. We cannot deny that the first may have taken priority over the second little by little as people worked out the idea of creation as distinct from simple making. Alarmed by the implications, instead of giving them a place in their own souls, believers preferred to project them into the beyond, where there lived by then a benevolent and covenanting deity, quite different from those merciless and jealous gods on Olympus.

What I have called a 'theological deformation' has shifted the idea of creation from an act corresponding to a limited kind of fashioning, which restores what time erases, which governs the rotation of things, to a revolutionary act, part of an irreversible process of mutation and betterment, where that which did not exist is brought into being.

In speaking about an artistic or intellectual creator, we rehabilitate creation as a human activity, in fact, as human growth *par excellence*. At the same time we notice that it is necessary to rescue it from the unilateral connotation of an exclusively positive act. Such a simplification is prevalent so long as creativity is lodged in the bosom of God, which Christian doctrine has made exclusively good. In returning creation to humanity we want instead to recover its roots in passion, solitude and, in a larger sense, in the difficulties and losses of the soul.

And so, just as each plant sprouts from dung and soil, each birth occurs amidst pain and blood. Human creation is not accompanied by triumphal marches, but instead by disjointed sounds and silences.

Let us try putting it somewhat differently. Contemporary civilization, in contrast to earlier epochs, advances its own development not in theological terms but in those of anthropology, not as a *donum dei*, but as human growth. Creation is undergoing an 'anthropological restoration', a humanistic closure of the cycle in which humanity turns towards God. In this sense, creation in the psyche reveals a divine resource within the human subject. But as human beings are flawed and sickness-ridden, unlike God, the root of creation always comes freighted with subjective suffering, and the link between this origin point and the creative response, a period of time either left fallow or tilled in solitary by the poet (14), gradually finds its way into historical and psychoanalytic work.

Therefore we are only looking more closely into and rendering more organic a fact observed by many others: namely, that creation is not an ever-flowing stream but an eruption preceded by silence and apparent inactivity.

Henri Ellenberger, author of the most complete study of the origins of depth psychology (15), accentuating initial concepts from romantic medicine, has introduced and elaborated the idea of a 'creative illness' in order to explain, in corresponding biographical terms, the evolution of the work of Freud, Jung, Nietzsche and Fechner (16). According to this idea, in the illness (or more precisely in that state of productive blockage and existential disorientation which in extraordinary personalities is poorly labeled as depression) one observes no simple decline nor even the kind of suffering that mobilizes the powers of recovery for a return to the original state. Conversely, a radical occasion for growth and deliverance occurs, at whose end the individual has not restored the condition prior to the illness but has established himself at a higher level.

In contrast to the productivity of those values to which we are accustomed, misfortune here receives a positive estimation. It constitutes not the final stage of a diminishment but the initial occasion for an expansion. In a similar manner the state of solitude, which contemporary social atavism devalues, is not the final moment of abandonment but the inaugural phase of rediscovering that greatest of presences, the divine, or at least the creator's own element, different from the ego, yet in modern terms its extension.

If contempt for the world and disenchantment with it have deprived us of the sound of God's word and of the apparitions of his image, the corresponding feeling does not erase itself, but becomes evermore private, isolated from the hubbub and the spectacle with which the mass media refills the theological void.

In a poem by Rilke called '*Herbst*' ('Autumn'), the whole earth drops from the sky into darkness and solitude. God is no longer a celestial omnipresence, but the invisible hand which manages this migration downward. God is this descent rather than a lifting-up.

The modern religious experience is rather antithetical to the stir the world makes about it while fleeing from it. *'Religion is what the individual does with his own solitariness...and if you are never solitary you are never religious'* (18; original italics). Transformed in such a manner, religious experience loses its connotations of an encounter with the universal, the glorious and the all-powerful. Instead it is the lonely experience of a restricted condition. The fruit of an existential dead-end, of sequestration, finite in time and confined strictly to interiority, it is also that way in consciousness. Whoever puts this to the test will not succeed in knowing whether the living encounter that overcomes the blockage is only the metaphor of an interior movement or else corresponds to the manifestation of a being already present.

In other words, the 'creative invalid' who recovers the use of his limbs after being paralyzed, and mislays the event, fails to recognize that in the world as it is today his psychological reactivation corresponds to a theological event. He does not know whether he has recovered 'creativity' within himself or the individual spark which the Creator has lodged in him.

Set over against those periods in which Christianity governed every aspect of life and the artist felt himself moulded by divine inspiration, at the moment when this man's feeling is possessed by rather exclusively religious themes it is infinitely more solitary and therefore (applying Whitehead again), in a seeming paradox, more deeply religious.

More than with the traditional Christian, in solitude the contemporary creative character is close to her cousin of the pre-Christian era. In opposition to the Judeo-Christian world, where God is good and just, where humanity is created in his image in order to populate the earth and where Christ is the great exemplar, divinity is classical polytheism neither showing itself to be good nor asking to be imitated.

In the words of Herodotus, it was *phthóneron te kai terakodes*, envious and turbulent (*The Histories,* I.32): happiness, beauty and creative possibilities were guarded without being allotted to human beings, save on occasion and for limited periods of time. Every attempt to attain a good thing for the first time and to keep it for good, as in the case of Prometheus, was punished by divine jealousy.

Ever since Western monotheism first chose a single people and then the whole of humanity as the vessel for its word and its images, to lend scope to history and institute faith in improvement, mankind has felt itself invited to produce, to win souls, to conquer worlds and realms of knowledge, and to believe in progress. In our current society also, Western humanity, even though God has withdrawn from its world of values, somewhat compulsively repeats this movement of expansion and growth (*cre*-scita or growing-ness). That idea points, again and again, to the renewed channeling of omnipotent creation (*cre*-azione or growth activity).

For their part, the peoples of the Orient and the global South can call on no alternatives to leading their own civilizations through a gradual devolution which leaves them to be reshaped along Western lines, rehearsing the relationship already worked out between Yahweh and his

Judeo-Christian Adam. Actually, the positivist, secular and technical world is the half-conscious continuator of an optimistic Christian inspiration, to the extent that it looks towards the assets and beliefs of improvement and progress, while at the same time negating the complexity of Christian values and the great religions, which have lent meaning also to grief, evil and death.

Illness, suffering and death for today's secular world are not presences which one can dialectically question and engage with when probing for meanings, but are simply absences: the disappearance, respectively, of health, well-being and life. As noted, while at one time people died at home exchanging important words with their own kin, today one dies in a hospital behind a screen; the dying person is no longer a subject who imparts instructions and wisdom at the moment of greatest solemnity, but simply the object of medical manipulation. Therapeutic relentlessness overrides the simplest limit, set in place by nature. The unquestioned mythology of progress comes down to metastasizing technical applications and continuous innovation, made thick by the fear of every form of emptiness. Acquisition takes on a meaning, while it can still clutch at it, construed solely in terms of how much space it fills. Death too wears out its meaning when, instead of passage, it simply becomes the loss of life.

Let us now recast this discussion as an outline, selecting themes for the paradoxical specificity which today circumscribes the creative process.

On one side is the secularization of society and the waning of Christianity as a universally shared practice. These two factors deprive the creative personality of a traditional affiliation with God, restoring to the word 'creation' a weaker, intransitive meaning, like the original one that was homologous to 'growth'. In behaving this way, they heave it into a double solitude: into unexplored territory where whoever creates something no longer has the Creator as a guide, and, beyond that, into a still latent pre-Christian superstition, where the gods turned suspicious and jealous in the face of any happy human achievement.

On the other side we meet emerging forms of artistic and cultural sensibility which give attention to the creative process as a fact in its own right, making fully evident its aspect of complexity.

The growth of consciousness, in every society whose available wealth in the broad sense is cultural, has produced an unprecedented estimation of creative processes in themselves, viewed no longer as theophanies of the Creator, or as chapters internal to an artistic movement, or simply as a necessary stage in the continuity of a technological process. Since depth psychology plays a central role in this critical consciousness, creativity as an indissoluble unity has been progressively based, in clinical outline as well, on its moments of immobility before an obstruction, of prolonged emptiness and long-suffering latency, after which the new result flows forth (creative illness).

Still a third aspect is the culture of progress which, now universally dominant, instead limits the vision of creativity within the 'complex' aspect just referred to. Ever increasingly, in fact, the culture of progress disparages all the voids and losses, the reflective pause or the sadness which to all appearances is unproductive. It additionally dismisses those meanings which rise from the experience of limitation and of death itself, whose natural prototype it is. In such a unilateral spirit it artificially dissociates the unity of the creative process, out of which it plucks only the final, acquisitive aspect. Cut off from its origins and from the fact of process, creation then is like lighting a lamp where there is no darkness, or providing food in the absence of hunger or appetite, or like a journey that consists in arriving without either leaving or traveling.

If we reconsider the creative process in its complexity we shall be able instead to argue that, in contrast to divine creation, which brings things into being without declaring either purpose or motive, human creation always has a starting point: the response to an obstacle which is not restricted to surmounting or annulling it, in which case we would speak merely of adaptation or readjustment. At the end of a response to such obstructions, there definitely remains in hand for the human being a creation (*cre-azione*, growth action) or, more modestly and etymologically, a growth (*cre-scita*, growing-ness).

This way of conceiving creation—which seizes its origin from the obstruction while suffering, derives its purpose from affirming a specifically human confrontation with the obstacle, and derives meaning from the excess left over in response (whether divine spark or civic benefit)—can propose itself as a point of equilibrium between two biased visions. To the right is the theological one, historically obsolete, in which every end is already catalogued and preordained in the divine mind, which leaves humanity able to discover, but not to create. On the left is a secular materialism in which the human mind, though creative, is subjected to various causes but is not mobilized by ultimate ends, a vision more in keeping with techno-scientific exigencies, but which fails to inquire into the meaning of creation.

In order to show the significance and topicality of this process model of obstacle-creation, we shall refer to the function which analogous models would play either in the historical sciences or in depth psychology.

In his twelve-volume *A Study of History*, Arnold Toynbee has produced the most famous and monumental attempt at reading universal history (18). According to Toynbee, the key and chief explanation for the genesis of all civilizations is the dynamic of *challenge-response*. Civil society is born wherever natural conditions or the pressures of a confined population set human beings a challenge, to which their creativity reacts successfully (19). Naturally this dynamic validates itself only under certain conditions. If the challenge is moderate it fails to focus the mind, as in many tropical regions where nature insures a constant level of food and adequate temperatures. If the challenge is overwhelming the response nearly exhausts itself in its attempts at securing the conditions for survival, as has happened with the Inuit.

A creative challenge-response, leading to civilization, is visible in Greece, where the extremely mountainous and jagged terrain welcomed inhabitants only on a restricted scale, prompting travel and discovery, and produced various kinds of gains but always in limited areas, stimulating the Greeks to find new ways to conduct business, monetary exchange, overland and maritime transport, and the handling of commodities.

This is not the place to dwell on this much debated, indisputably rich theme, to the extent that Ortega did in severely criticizing *A Study of History* whilst singing its praises (20). We can get away with noting a certain analogy to the Darwinian model, advanced by Toynbee himself: just as the most versatile species (human beings and rodents) are prepared to respond to every environment while the more specialized species go extinct (prehistoric animals), so too those civilizations which have developed the greatest number of possible cultural aspects have endured (Athens, according to the celebrated epitaph of Pericles) while those which have concentrated on only one have vanished (Sparta and its monoculture of war).

What is most worthy of underlining about the creation of civilizations in our little sketch is its way of moving past zero. Human beings react to a circumstantial challenge with a response that is not limited to canceling it out, but additionally to furnishing a creation or growth that constitutes the seed of the entire development of civilization.

Turning our attention now to depth psychology, let us close with the most original concept of symbolization in the field, namely Jung's. In contrast to Freud, for whom the symbol is the concealment of a censored reality (for example, a sexual organ in the imagery of a dream), for Jung the symbol is to be welcomed as an original unconscious product endowed with its own value. It cannot be translated into something else, into an object that must be individuated retroactively; it constitutes the best representation of a reality which can be rendered in no other terms. According to Jung, that which Freud called the symbol is in reality a sign, a conventional image which exhausts all of its functions in pointing to something else. (To revert to our earlier formulation, it is a zero-sum game.) The Jungian symbol, on the contrary, corresponds to an autonomous creation of the psyche, complex and never subject to an exhaustive analysis. It plays the role of a 'transcendent function'. That is, caught by a neurosis and tied up in ambivalence, the subject often gets a fresh start not by working out conscious choices, which ambivalence by definition prevents, but by intuiting a third way, a synthesis of two blocked paths brought about by the symbol that transcends them both by installing itself on a higher level (or, if you will, a deeper one). On that plane, as one may sense intuitively, the kinship between the concepts of *syn-thesis* and *sym-bol* is not at all that fortuitous. For this reason, likewise available to intuition, Jungian analysis does not aim so much at dismantling and decoding the symbol as it does at valorizing it, so as to ride the wave of psychic energy which generally goes with it (for example in the eruption of particularly emotional dream images).

We needn't even go beyond such a case. Rather, staying with our task it is fitting to note that, unlike Freud's, the Jungian symbol is no zero-sum game but an additive and definitive creation that does not vanish upon revealing a hidden truth, nor, to the extent that it reconciles two antinomian factors, is it content to be their algebraic sum but rises above them, creating a new fact.

Corresponding to this theoretical conception is a clinical attitude that rejects as inadequate the therapy which aims simply at restoring health (a zero-sum game between illness and cure) and, going beyond the same idea of *healing* more than a generation before anti-psychiatry, proposes the model of *individuation*; a unique structure that cannot be programmed, in which the encounter with psychic illness is the challenge that moves one to actualize one's own potentialities, and the indicator that shows the illness not as a presence to be done away with, but as an absence of what the person can be or can grow in himself. Once again we meet the productive residual, that creation which the "sufferer" firmly carries into the light by responding to the suffering.

In a civilization that profanes and eradicates every kind of limitation, above all suffering and death, creation as a response to limits and obstacles works not only to overcome them, but promotes a new meaning that restores value to the painful experience of living.

Presented to the conference on *Ill-being and Creation* in Milan, 1988, and published with the conference papers.

(14) Undoubtedly, since already with Homer part of Odysseus's creative intelligence is born out of enforced exile and his longing to return to far-off Ithaca, regardless of how hard it is to determine when the hero's intelligence is his own and when it obeys the promptings of the goddess Athene.
(15) Henri Ellenberger, *TheDiscovery of the Unconscious: The History and Evolution of Dynamic Psychiatry.* Basic Books, New York, 1970.
(16) *Ibid.*, pp. 447-448, 672-673, *et passim.*
(17) Alfred North Whitehead, *Religion in the Making.* Cambridge University Press, London, 1926, p.16.
(18) Oxford University Press, Oxford 1934 (1934-1961).
(19) *Ibid.*, especially Books II, III, IX and X.
(20) Ortega y Gasset, *An Interpretation of Universal History* (1966). Norton, New York 1973, Chapters X and XI.

Chapter Six

Analysis: Growth or Cure?

To grow: ...come naturally into existence; arise, originate, develop (as from a seed)... Of a living thing: increase gradually in size, length, or height by natural development; ...come or pass by degrees (in)to some state or condition.
To cure: ... treat surgically or medically. Restore to health, relieve of an illness, an evil. Heal (an illness, a wound); remedy, remove (an evil).
(*The New Shorter Oxford English Dictionary*, 1993 ed.)

The subject of these reflections is the epistemological arrogance of *psychodynamics* which, often seduced by the veneration accorded to the natural sciences, asserts itself as a repository of scientific truths. I would like to suggest that such an assertion be interpreted analytically: that is to say, through a study of its unconscious motivations, in line with the principal application of psychodynamics. After all, as the study of envy constitutes an important application of psychodynamics, it here inspires a legitimate suspicion: namely, that given its own limited prestige, psychodynamics may well envy the universal prestige of medicine.

We insist at times, out of force of habit, on thinking of Freud as a neurologist, a navigator who, in the wake of his explorations, established psychodynamics in a medical context. Actually, as his compatriot Stefan Zweig had already intuited in 1931:

The fact that Freud happened to topple the Chinese wall of old psychological conceptions from a medical point of departure is, yes, historically correct, but not relevant as far as results go. In a creative personality, the point of origin is not as relevant as the direction or the point to which one pushes oneself. It does not matter that Freud's starting point was medicine, just as it does not matter that Pascal's starting point was mathematics, or that Nietzsche's was ancient philology. (21)

The gynaecologist and the pediatrician

In the early 1990s, two issues of the *American Journal of Psychiatry* (vols. 147 & 148) and a response to these which appeared in *Psicoterapia e scienze umane* (vol. 3) described how the celebrated Chestnut Lodge Clinic was ordered to pay compensatory damages to a depressed patient who had undergone extensive analysis with no remission of his symptoms. Immediately afterward, in another institution, the symptoms were successfully and rapidly treated with medication. I mention this extreme case not so much for the misleading and lone result that it describes, but for what I see as its faulty premise and as a basis for general discussion.

What had been promised to the patient before treatment? And what was the premise on which treatment was based? Apparently, the patient had been promised that he would be directed in the best way possible towards recovery ('to direct' does not mean to reach the goal, but to chart a course to be followed). Just as apparently, the idea of recovery adhered closely to the traditional medical model, whereby sanity was to be restored as quickly and completely as possible. Was the institution overstepping its bounds in making such a commitment? While none of us witnessed the analytic work done, on the basis of information made public one might argue that it did not consist of alleviating the patient's suffering. To the contrary, the work consisted of bringing to light serious unconscious suffering.

It is not my intention to suggest that psychoanalysis is uninterested in fighting a patient's symptoms or suffering. In a broad sense, and as any discipline concerned with human life, psychodynamics certainly aims to help people. In a specific sense, however, it has as its goal—rather, as its central value—the transformation and growth of people whose personalities, prior to analysis, may have been hindered by unidentifiable psychological factors. Whereas for psychoanalysis the elimination of symptoms is only a desirable and welcome consequence, for traditional medicine it is the end, for which transformation and psychodynamic growth are but means.

'But', a slightly impatient outsider might object, 'indirectly you pursue the same end as medicine. The bottom line is that you're paid to alleviate symptoms'. But no. Exactly for this reason it is ethically and epistemologically wrong for the analyst to promise the patient a fight against symptoms or the restoration of health. The symptom is a companion, which may well accompany the very transformation which the analyst ought to facilitate. The recovery of a previous state (*cure*) is not in the analytical order of things, for after a transformation the patient will be in a new condition which cannot be known beforehand.

Consider the following basic example. The burst of sexuality at adolescence is often accompanied by problems of uncontrollable emotionality, insomnia, difficulty concentrating, radical oppositional views, etc. What will the objectives of the analyst be when the parents of such an adolescent seek help for their child? More than any other phase of life, adolescence is characterized by transformation; thus, to strive for recovery, or a 'cure', at such a time becomes nonsensical if by recovery one means a return to a psychic state that preceded the disturbance. As the very word suggests, psychodynamics must privilege movement (dynamics) rather than a return to a previous equilibrium or the defence of an already existing one. Recovery, however, commonly understood as a return to equilibrium, might thus be termed 'psychostatic'.

Certainly the analyst and medical doctor must work closely together when treating an adolescent. The former must try to foster the adolescent's growth toward an adult sexual identity, while the latter must intervene pharmacologically if any symptom becomes unbearable or weakens the body. These two specialists, however, have different aims and different interpretative models. On the one hand, the medical doctor pursues a cure, which can usually be verified objectively in the short term; only indirectly does he or she pursue growth. The analyst, on the other hand, seeks long-term growth — validated above all else by the patient's subjective feelings; only indirectly is a cure sought in any traditional sense. Herein lies the error of Chestnut Lodge: the psychological intervention, based on values which were foreign to it, was a failure in terms of the medical model, which the institution itself used to describe the case. In this sense, there was no clinical error, but an epistemological one.

Interestingly, the article in the *American Journal of Psychiatry* suggests that, in addition to the quick pharmacological cure (or remission of the more serious symptoms), the personality of the patient also experienced long-term benefits of a maturational kind. As in most analogous cases, the patient's misfortunes present a tangled web of suffering, in which the organic component is very difficult to extricate from the psychic one. However, if we were able to distinguish between them, we might conceive of the organic condition as largely reversible. Not so for the psychodynamic condition; as everyone knows, the birth of a child, or the sudden prospect of a new job, can set off anxiety crises or depression in the same person who, ten years later, adequately mature, would react to the same event with serenity and satisfaction. Unlike bodily growth, psychological growth can take place in adults as well, and protect a person definitively from certain kinds of suffering.

To return to the case of our adolescent, his main symptoms may well disappear in a short period of time. Yet, if this happens, the analyst would do well to remember that her objective is of a different order: namely, to foster the growth of adult sexual identity, or the transformation of boy into man. This process will inevitably last a long time and will be judged not by the disappearance of suffering, but by the appearance of a personality that is substantially new. Whereas cure returns to us something that was, growth turns up something new.

Moreover, because the disturbances that accompany adolescent maturation are more the rule than the exception, the analyst must wonder to what extent it is even appropriate to combat those disturbances. The adolescent faces a necessary passage, accompanied by necessary difficulties and suffering, which recall by analogy those of giving birth. The analyst, precisely because of her expertise in the insidiousness of the unconscious—and out of respect for that grave biblical pronouncement, 'In sorrow thou shalt bring forth children'—should not herself act unconsciously and sadistically. For to give birth (symbolically, to generate new life within oneself) *does* hurt. Alleviating pain is the right thing to do, as long as it does not conflict with the birth of the new.

To stick with the birthing metaphor, gynaecologist and pediatrician can work side by side in the delivery room, constantly reinventing their roles, even sacrificing something of their own respective aims, to make room for those of the other. By no means traitors to their respective professions in such a situation, these professionals can serve as an example. The analyst, like the pediatrician, is concerned with new, not earlier, life. She must foster birth and growth, not maintenance or restoration. Yet while the tasks of pediatrician and gynaecologist, or of analyst and medical doctor, can judiciously be harmonized, they must not be confused as one and the same.

The reduction of pain and the health of the mother (that is, the conservation of an earlier form of life) are not directly the pediatrician's domain, even if his intervention is well known to analysts who are also medical doctors and are familiar with both professions. When pharmacological intervention is warranted, it certainly cannot be rejected because of ideological prejudice or compartmentalization. In general, however, it is advisable to entrust this intervention to a colleague, so as not to embody split and divergent functions, and not to create correspondingly split expectations in the patient (i.e., a dissociated and ambivalent transference).

A Myth of Origins

At this point, I would like to clarify the values and attitude of the analytic model, as compared with those of the medical model. Analytic discipline—at least the Jungian one to which I refer—does not belong to the natural sciences. According to its viewpoint, much as psychic disturbance is not the ultimate obstacle to confront, so the causes of the disturbance are not of central concern. In other words, a disturbance is important not because of its origin but because of the end towards which the disturbance points. According to Jung:

> A neurosis is by no means merely a negative thing, it is also something positive. Only a soulless rationalism, reinforced by a narrow materialistic outlook, could possibly have overlooked this fact. In reality, the neurosis contains the patient's psyche, or at least an essential part of it; and if, as the rationalist pretends, the neurosis could be plucked from him like a bad tooth, he would have gained nothing, but would have lost something very essential to him. That is to say, he would have lost as much as the thinker deprived of his doubt, or the moralist deprived of his temptation, or the brave man deprived of his fear.

> To lose a neurosis is to find oneself without an object; life loses its point and hence its meaning. This would not be a cure, it would be a regular amputation; and it would be cold comfort indeed if the psychoanalyst then assured the patient that he had lost nothing but his infantile paradise, with its wishful chimeras, most of them perverse. Very much more would have been lost, for hidden in the neurosis is a bit of still undeveloped personality. (22)

The neurosis is part of the path to be followed. It is like Ariadne's thread which, unwittingly neglected, comes to us in the form of a tangled ball of yarn. To use another image, a neurotic disturbance is not so much a cumbersome weight to unload as that of a dark tunnel we must pass through. Without the tunnel, we would remain on this side of an impassable mountain obstructing our life.

Let me give another example. A young man shows up for analysis in a state of profound depression. His life seems to have hit a dead-end. Still, his young career is going surprisingly well, and he is admired and well-liked for his creativity, integrity and sensitivity. The same seems to hold for his private life, where friends of both sexes seek him out. And yet he feels lonely. He does not know what to do with all the affection and success. More generally, he does not know what he wants from life.

From the first sessions his dreams confront us with images of homosexuality. His childhood seems typical of this sort of problem: a closed and authoritarian father, and an overprotective, castrating mother. The patient is already aware of this aspect of his nature, even if he has never made room for it in his day-to-day life. Yet the simple signs in this fairly common case are enough to raise a series of questions. How far should we go in trying to discover the causes of his homosexuality? Is it fair to promise the patient that we will fight, with all available means, the suffering presently afflicting him? Additionally, if he does not know what he really wants from life, will the patient be satisfied to know what he really wants from sex?

Keeping to the distinction between the medical and psychodynamic models (between *cure* and *growth*), we can attempt some answers. We often attribute great importance to psychological causes lying in a patient's past, not because we have verified their effects, but because we attribute to such processes of verification an importance derived from the dominant model of the natural sciences, that is to say, of medicine itself. Science is the kingdom of causes; and in today's disillusioned and hero-less world, on a shrunken planet bereft of surprises, we have come to mythologize the scientist, in his quest for knowledge, as the last true explorer; as the last true combatant, now that wars and warriors have proven too destructive; as the last true saint, now that religious belief has surrendered to secular thought.

The scientist is, in all likelihood, the mythologem underlying every esteemed activity of modernity. It is they who fight to recover the origins of observed phenomena, much as Odysseus fought to return to his family and reconquer the land of his childhood; or as St Francis struggled to rediscover the simplicity that was lost by the wealthy and educated of his day. An origin could be Ithaca, or harmony with nature, or the source of a physical phenomenon: realities which, while different from one another, are all united by our conviction that whoever regains the origin will be honoured as a hero.

Let us not mistake, then, the role of case histories in analysis. Of course patients should recount their childhoods, but mainly because retelling the past stirs up great emotions in the present. Strong feelings can jolt a blocked life into motion and restore the promise of a future. What matters, though, is building symbols in the present, not reconstructing a road already taken: 'Hateful to me', writes Goethe, 'is all that merely instructs me, without immediately enhancing or enlivening my work' (23). Hardly any of us today needs to reach Ithaca, nor would anyone get there via the senseless course charted by Homer. And yet, people the world over continue to read the *Odyssey*, because Ulysses' return home holds a message for any persons in search of themselves.

Strictly speaking then, causality alone, applied to the psyche, is of little help. For example, parents like those of my patient (authoritarian father, overprotective mother) also generate incurable Don Juans as often as they do obsessively loyal spouses; they can as readily produce people satisfied with their life choices as they can a son, like my patient, dissatisfied with and afflicted by his existence. Even interpretations like 'latent' homosexuality, used to explain situations like my patient's, are ultimately based on weak causal links: often enough their very wording defines the origin being sought, as well as the cure to propose to the patient for the condition thus established (24). More than a form of knowing, this is a form of tautology.

True, *those* parents did generate *that* son. However, the analyst cannot know the parents' uniqueness, only a patterned account brought by the patient that *may* be applicable to other situations. The analyst might not recognize a patient's parents at all if he were suddenly to cross paths with them in real life—even if they are the same beings who have been described for years. As doubts set in and threaten to chip away retroactively at years of work, the bewildered therapist may ask: 'To what degree did my patient knowingly lie to me, or did his memory delude him? And why did my work, based on such grossly distorted premises, nonetheless help him on a course of deep personal discovery, in the course of a successful analysis?'

The reactions of the human psyche are marked more by uniqueness than by causality. Even patients' accounts of their lives do not escape this rule, as the accounts themselves become symbolic worlds, independent of both narrator and the ensemble of characters described. For instance, it can be very difficult for an analyst, who happens to accept for treatment the brother of an ex-patient, to recognize the same family of origin.

At this point, it will have become clear that, if I have reduced to three the questions raised by our patient—concerning past causes, present suffering and future possibilities—it has been to shift emphasis gradually from the first question to the third. Psychodynamics must move (*dynamic*) with life as it unfolds; it cannot insist on backward glances. To look backwards—that is, to base one's knowledge primarily on trodden paths—maximizes the risk of not identifying a false path *en route* to the future. Where the life of the emotions is concerned, the risk is being led to a narcissistic microcosm: to a life of recounting one's own myth of origins, in an ongoing, personal celebration of the liturgy of a Paradise Lost. While an assessment of present-day options creates in people a capacity for the exercise of responsibility (and therefore *growth*), focusing on a patient's infancy institutionally 'invents' (from the Latin *invenire*, to find) an infantile patient.

Life is frequently unpleasant, but it is not through a return to Eden that we can make it better. In keeping with this biblical image, we might remember that Yahweh, after chasing his offspring from the Earthly Paradise, also promised them redemption: not in the form of a return, however, but of a going beyond. In the same way are cure and growth differentiated: on the one hand, by concerning itself with past events, and by proposing a return to what has already been experienced, cure determines its goals and parameters in advance; growth, by contrast, is open-ended, tending towards that which is possible and individually diversified. In sum, cure can be objectively verified and pertains to the natural sciences. Growth depends on personal experience. Being understood in this way, analysis enhances the personality, and the patient who uses it grows.

But analysis should also be warned against pursuing extraneous ways to knowledge. Analysis' own epistemological arrogance has often fostered the very mythic ailments it proposes to cure (structured, for example, around the myths of Narcissus and Oedipus). Years of gazing inward can favour a patient's narcissism, while a prolonged dependence on the analyst may well reactivate Oedipal experiences. Similarly, the omnipotence of the past, (the power of an origin myth, or of the analytic cosmogony) encourages causal links which analysts may then be tempted to apply through interpretation. In both cases, the intended object of analysis (mythic thought) risks being inadvertently transformed into an active and deforming element of the analytic process itself.

The Cathedral and the Quarry

It is claimed that the most common error of psychodynamics is not its limited therapeutic efficacy—we already know that analysis has more to do with consciousness than with cure—but its efforts to incorporate the medical model as a permanent, structural element of its own. For while this model has influenced the origins of the discipline over a century ago in the office of a Viennese neurologist, psychoanalysis is not a science: not, at least, in the sense ascribed to the natural sciences. Psychodynamics is concerned with specific and unique events, not with events predetermined by fixed laws; indeed its applications have little to do with what can be known in advance. But such considerations do not deny its value as an important form of knowledge, as a heuristic tool capable of yielding general yet reliable insights into the course of a human life.

Nobody of course would deny the importance of history. Yet despite the fact that we speak of historical sciences, history too deals only with singular, unrepeatable events. While history can propose to study the origins of such events, it can never truly predict the events themselves; nor can a historian make any generalizations about their nature, unlike the chemist or physicist who relies on causal models to predict a succession of events. We must, in any case, be sure to clarify what we mean by *origin*: do we mean a beginning in time or a causal principle? The verb *orio*, from which the word *origin* is derived, does not distinguish between the two. A Latin word, *orio* is much older than modern-day scientific discourse and any resultant distinctions of this kind.

Even today we continue, almost superstitiously, to make use of terms that unify temporal and causal succession, infusing the former with something of the force of the latter (maybe, in the case of analysts or historians, to move closer to the natural sciences.) While this was, admittedly, more evident in languages of old, residues do persist. Consider, for example, the Greek *arche*, denoting principles both of temporality and of agency. The word's ambivalence is, in fact, still at the root of words like archaeology (study of a past with limited influence, if any, on the present) and archetype (a past 'type' still active in determining a type in the present). Allow me, on this score, to cite a historian whose words, I believe, can also be applied to psychodynamics (that is, to the deep history of an individual): 'In any study, seeking the origins of a human activity, there lurks the same danger of confusing ancestry with explanation' (25). Earlier in the same passage, the historian resorts to an image to explain the same idea: 'Great oaks from little acorns grow. But only if they meet favorable conditions of soil and climate, conditions which are entirely beyond the scope of embryology'(26).

If this kind of unpredictable, individual growth is true for plant life, is it not all the more true for human life? The human element introduces an inexhaustible multiformity, yielding uniquenesses that cannot be replicated. If I were asked, for example, about the origin of Milan's cathedral, I might identify the quarries from which the stone was extracted. In this way, however, through a limited understanding of the word 'origin', I would only have specified the church's chemical-geological basis, at the expense of its architectural qualities—a feature which everyone, including the chemist and the geologist, admires as the cathedral's defining characteristic. To give meaning to the structure, therefore, is to see it not only in its chemical context but in its cultural context as well, where countless psychological elements—neither predictable nor replicable—are constellated and come into play. As Marc Bloch states:

> Historical facts are, in essence, psychological facts.... To be sure, human destinies are placed in the physical world and suffer the consequences thereof. Even where the intrusion of these external forces seems most brutal, however, their action is weakened or intensified by man and his mind.(27)

Earlier in the same passage Bloch argues:

> Historical meaning in contemporary practice does not differ in its procedure. However necessary they may be, the most constant and general antecedents remain merely implicit. What military historian would dream of ranking among the causes of a victory that gravitation which accounts for the trajectory of the shells, or the physiological organization of the human body without which the projectiles would have no fatal consequences?. . . What is the use of dwelling upon nearly universal antecedents? They are common to too many phenomena to deserve a special niche in the genealogy of any of them. I am well aware, from the onset, that there would be no fire if the air contained no oxygen: what interests me, what demands and justifies an attempt at discovery, is to determine how the fire started. The laws of trajectories are as valid for defeat as for victory: they explain both; therefore they are useless as a proper explanation for either.(28)

So it is for human beings, to the extent that we can reverse Bloch's statement and claim: 'Psychic facts are the facts of history; that is to say, they are the individual histories of psychic life'. Like the histories of peoples, psychic facts are also bound by fixed rules, both physical and chemical. No one would deny as much. Yet for the analyst, such antecedents remain, for the most part, implied, since they do not aid the comprehension of what is at the heart of psychodynamic investigation: namely, the individual specificity of psychic life which, while never identical to that of any other human being, is also never identical to itself over time (precisely because of its *dynamic* quality). As in the human sciences, the study of antecedents is useful insofar as it promotes comprehension; it cannot, however, provide us with definitive formulas for understanding. The veneration of origins is a necessity of the human mind, exercised for millennia in all cultures, including today's secular, Western societies. It is exemplified throughout the study of myth, as in the story of Ulysses' return to Ithaca. In this light, we can see how even psychodynamics' obsessive exaltation in the case-history method, induced by the parasitical use of causal models, is no stranger to mythic forms of unconscious survival. But a psychodynamics configured in the context of the human (and not the natural) sciences will have to come to grips with this regressive temptation. Interestingly enough, historians have already performed this epistemological self-criticism, distancing themselves in the process from a method whose cult of origins is often exposed as a cult of the dead.

This turning point, finally, was already prefigured by Nietzsche, who contributed significantly to its articulation both as a critic of history and as a proto-psychologist:

> Thus: it is possible to live almost without memory, and to live happily moreover, as the animal demonstrates; but it is altogether impossible to *live* at all without forgetting. Or, to express my theme even more simply: *there is a degree of sleeplessness, of rumination, of the historical sense, which is harmful and ultimately fatal to the living thing, whether this living thing be a man or a people or a culture* (29).

Or, as he continues:

> When the past speaks, it always speaks as an oracle: only if you are an architect of the future and know the present will you understand it.... If you look ahead and set yourself a great goal, you at the same time restrain that rank analytical impulse which makes the present into a desert and all tranquility, all peaceful growth and maturing, almost impossible (30).

Nietzsche aimed these reflections at both the individual and society. Underlying them is an epistemology that privileges, in either case, the dynamics of the psyche. For history, in its own right, is not simply a list of past and unmodifiable events, but a search (*istoria*): a trying and, of necessity, an incomplete *construction of the meaning(s) of those very events*. Consequently, the parameters which we use to evaluate history are not based on what has already happened, but on what is yet to come. Like the parameters of growth—as opposed to those of cure—they reside in the future, not in the past. For those among us who want to grow, the past exists to the extent that it can be overcome.

This essay was first published in English in Anthony Molino and Christine Ware, eds., *Where Id Was*. New York, Continuum, 2001, Chapter 6, pp. 61-72 (translation by the editors).

(21) Stefan Zweig, *Die Heilung durch den Geist: Mesmer, Mary Baker-Eddy, Freud.* Frankfurt, Fischer, 1982 (author's translation from the German).
(22) C.G. Jung, 'The State of Psychotherapy Today', in *Collected Works* vol. X. Princeton, Princeton University Press, 1970, p. 355.
(23) Goethe, letter to Schiller, 19 December 1798 (author's translation from the German).
(24) This is a strong argument in support of Karl Popper's theory of the unfalsifiability of analysis. See his *Conjectures and Refutations: The Growth of Scientific Knowledge.* New York, Basic Books, 1962.
(25) Marc Bloch, *The Historian's Craft.* New York, Alfred A. Knopf, 1953, p. 32. Translation from the French by Peter Putnam.
(26) *Ibid.*, p. 32.
(27) *Ibid.*, p. 194.
(28) *Ibid.*, pp. 191-2
(29) Friederich Nietzsche, *Untimely Meditations.* New York, Cambridge University Press, 1983, p. 62. Translated by R.J. Hollingdale (italics in original).
(30) *Ibid.*, p. 94.

Chapter Seven

The Need for Growth

Instinct alone does not lead human beings to grow. Animals come into the world relatively self-sufficient, needing only to wait for the instincts already available to them to go into action. But for us, human growth is far more than a matter of physically consolidating needs and letting them go on running. It means knowing, understanding, learning and being aware. It is the weaving together of physical growth—almost invariable since *homo sapiens* first appeared—with a psychic growth capable of redoubling its complexity and mixing up its forms from one generation to the next. Science can pass judgment on the first matter, but only opinions can be pronounced about the rest.

Nevertheless, staying with the question of complexity, it is not accurate to say that humanity has utterly removed itself from instinct. Rather, it has transposed the functional model of instinct into the novel form of growth which encompasses knowing and awareness. It has transformed momentary curiosity into a permanent kind of drive. Knowledge has become the stable object of a desire that we resist only in exceptional cases, and to which it now and then yields, such as erotic desire or, better and more fundamentally, hunger. The extraordinary popularity of the figure of Ulysses applies here in every way. But if this is a matter concerning a transfer of instinct, it nonetheless amounts to a degeneration which transcends its origin, becoming omnipotent and therefore sick, as well as occasionally self-destructive. Ulysses withstands hunger and all kinds of hardship, but not, however, his need to know how far to venture into the Cyclops's cave (*Odyssey* IX).

This episode contains something much more complicated than the customary duel between heroes and villains. Ulysses puts in at the island of the Cyclops, whom the poet describes in a few bold strokes; foremost among his traits, he lacks all respect for the gods and the law, and feeds freely on wild animals and the fruits of the earth. The Greeks see a simple and enormous cave, the home of Polyphemus, son of Poseidon. They would simply like to pilfer food and make an escape, but Ulysses objects. More than hunger, the need to discover things guides him. When Cyclops comes home he proves to be violent, devouring his guests, whom Greeks customarily hold sacred. Ulysses, however, has devised a plan. Looking ahead, he has brought with him some of the very best wine, the gift of a priest of Apollo. It proves easy to get the monster dead drunk, and once Polyphemus has fallen fast asleep, it also becomes a simple matter to kill him. But for Ulysses this opportunity serves instead to harness the giant's force to remove the stone which the Cyclops has rolled across the mouth of his cave. By themselves the Greeks could never manage to dislodge it, and would remain prisoners.

If Ulysses embodies the curiosity that establishes a striving for knowledge, the Cyclops represents instinct in its naturally raw, loutish state. The man who sets out to master an endless kind of learning cannot let himself kill off such energy; he will make do with possessing this natural force—the energy of instinct—when he is hungry. He wants to get to know it because it is so fascinating. So he has to intoxicate, blind, and finally subordinate this vitality to his own ends, much as the drive toward civilization does, in putting the bridle on instinct and making it into the mount for its own permanent curiosity. Yet this adventure costs Ulysses his best men, and draws down on him the wrath of Poseidon, which inflicts further shipwreck on them. He will return to Ithaca alone. All his companions perish; not even the conquest of Troy cost them as dearly as did this drive of his to gain knowledge.

Greek mythology brings forth endless admonitions against the danger of the indomitable desire to seek knowledge. One of the most famous is found in Sophocles's *King Oedipus*. A simplistic popularization has it that Oedipus's problem is sexual, and that the king's implacable adversary is his own father Laius. As we shall see in a later chapter (31), the protagonist of this myth is possessed less by a sexual need—present in other myths but irrelevant here—than by an insatiable need to know. Oedipus nourishes no rivalry with Laius, a character whom he comes up against without knowing him and kills straight off before encountering Jocasta, and therefore not out of jealousy but in fulfillment of his destiny as a parricide. He himself is instead possessed by a mortal dislike of the seer Tiresias, whose clash with him occupies the central part of the drama.

Oedipus will find that his damnation comes not from a sexual urge, but rather from his desire to know his own origins at all costs (32). Tiresias represents a mode of knowing that is wise, grounded in mystery, and pays due respect to natural limits. Oedipus is instead a Ullysean, who sets against these attitudes a need to know things ultimately in depth; he is prophetically secular and enlightened. Tiresias possesses knowledge, but knows that it is better not to reveal it; he does not undo, in the name of rational simplifications, the complexity and ambivalence that come with a profound emotion, a symbol, or primary psychic experiences. Also here, the teaching of the myth about the curse of knowing is tremendous. Oedipus ridicules Tiresias for practicing the art of knowing whilst being blind. Nevertheless, when he comes to know what he had wanted to know, with symbolic acknowledgment he blinds himself. With his breathlessly insistent rationale, he thought he had come from far away; instead he had returned to the womb he left as an infant, and learnt that he married his mother. His curse is in itself incestuous, more in a cognitive way than a sexual one: his need to know does not conquer, or penetrate, a new space, but on the contrary curves back on itself towards origins.

Let us now return to growth. In the infant we observe a nutritive instinct securely overabundant and linked to a need for growth. It is evident that he feeds not simply to maintain his already achieved condition but seizes a proportionally greater amount of food than an adult, because he must go on growing his own body. But he always proceeds in cycles more or less marked by hunger and satiety; and with maturity the need to eat scales back and steadies itself. Hunger becomes self-limiting, no longer driven by the need to make the body grow. However, it is not that contrary cases are unknown, for they are classified as eating disorders, more precisely as bulimia.

Even on looking into its inner world, manipulating and exploring, the infant seems driven by a curiosity greater than needed in order to grow and, as we have said, it models itself analogously on instinct. With maturity, however, it does not stop itself. Very simply, growth becomes less manual and more cultural. Physical growth modulates into cognitive growth. The growth of knowledge transforms itself into an infinite accumulation.

The hunger to learn and know, therefore, is an instinct that has become persistently bulimic, out of control to the end of time. With it Ulysses contradicted the instinct for conservation, by setting life at risk for the sake of satisfying adolescent curiosity in an adult situation. Above all, such hunger fails to learn the alternation of need with satisfaction, because our psychic apparatus is a stomach that can be stretched almost infinitely. Besides, only in a simpler society strictly bound to the agricultural cycle (which Mircea Eliade calls the mythic model of Eternal Return) does the hunger for knowledge get inhibited in the adult phase so that it holds back from pursuing a cumulative improvement from generation to generation. It (the hunger) limits itself to the repetition of its own rituals and its own agricultural tasks or unvarying hunting practices. Not that all of this is sheer pattern-repetition exclusive of handy inventiveness and the courage that responds to novelty: consider such refined equipment as the boomerang devised by the Australian aborigines, or the discovery of America managed by the Vikings. Essentially, however, the presence of restrictive taboos prevails against curiosity and the need for betterment. To toss over the shoulder an entire way of being, to shake off a form of consolidated knowledge, is experienced rather as a blow than as an item of mere procedure.

In the alternative form of society, which has carried the day down to our own time, the necessity to achieve progress wins out. The "progressive" model of society has crushed the primordial model of static culture in the course of history. It has become absolutely natural with us to see every new kind of knowledge or consciousness not as a fact interesting or useful in itself, but as an element which inserts itself into an infinite series of improvements. The boomerang is not a gift from the ancestors whose design is faithfully handed down, but an interesting stage upon which we immediately seek to improve, in the march of launched and thrown implements. The discovery of America is a great step forward in the progress of geographical exploration, and so forth.

The infinitely accumulative model for growth has carried over in a permanent way into our psychological attitude. Naturally it is the new thing. The end has become the means. Any appetite for knowing had to serve the improvement of our knowledge, our quality of life, even rendering our moral existence more conscious of how we are and how we are with others, therefore more tolerant and more temperate. In the final reckoning, Ulysses stayed near the Cyclops's den because he wanted to know how to be something other than he was. Yet all that has transformed itself into a greedy because limitless hunger. That which was the self-perpetuation of an instinct on the plane of cognitive growth has turned into a strange and barely controllable obsession. The appetite for novelty in fact has no regard for persons, only for objects. We want trips to the moon and technical progress because we believe they make life better. Nevertheless, even if one day our earth does play host to different kinds of beings, we shall not take much interest in knowing them. From this point of view, even physical bulimia is no more than a particular case, undeniable because it is obvious in its symptoms, of a more general acquisitive bulimia. Persons affected by bulimia ceaselessly feed themselves, but often without the nerve even to try new dishes. This impulse is no different than the one which originally drives one to incorporate knowledge: in the infant the primary means of knowing things consists precisely in putting things into its mouth.

With this observation we are borrowing, for psychological purposes, an idea from ethology. The science of animal behaviour uses "neotony" (*neotema* in Italian, *Foetalizationstheorie* in German, and *jouvenilisme* in French) to identify the fixation of characteristics typical in the growth phase of an individual adult. This persistence of a state of 'perennial infancy' is in certain cases favoured by natural selection because it helps to insure the survival of the species. Just as in certain species - those who defend themselves better and therefore proliferate more - have the strongest teeth or tusks, so in others the favourites are those with the largest heads. Humans have the advantage of these larger cerebral dimensions not only because they possess them from birth, but also because these continue to expand for a longer time than in other species.

Given these reflections, even the layperson will have noticed how the human being is a profoundly neotonous animal. It is normally born with little hair and a relatively large, bulbous head. But only the human being remains that way into adulthood. At birth the brain of the chimpanzee is already almost full-sized, whereas the human brain must still enlarge itself nearly four times over. From a zoological viewpoint, therefore, the human being is a quadrumane fetus that reaches functional and sexual maturity. However, still more interesting from an organic aspect is the psychology of the neotonous human. An old stereotype has it that monkeys are inquisitive. In reality that is true of young monkeys but not of the grown-ups. The human, even in this sense, is the only perennially immature, perennially nosey monkey. This characteristic is so irrepressible that humankind, to live it out more completely, tops it off with projection. Humans attribute this feature, therefore, to all those animals they are somewhat similar to, like the monkey. Neoteny is the evolutionary and organic basis out of which floods that need we have called cultural bulimia.

If a 'pathology' is not an individual affair but something contrived by a whole civilization, at first it is inevitably more difficult to discern because it distorts the observer's outlook. To get some indirect notion, nevertheless, of how the spirit of the times is decisively complicit in psychic pathology, it is enough to run down a current list of analytical terms to realize that the generalized presence of an acquisitive instinct has metastasized into cancer: narcissism, omnipotence, grandiosity itself, psychopathy, psychic inflation, etc., as well as, on another level, what Freud had already prophesied as the 'discontents of civilization'. This is not all. Particularly since we have less to do with a psychology of individuals than with a civilizational illness, we clearly realize that many discussions which seem extraneous to psychology, such as 'the limits of development' and 'the end of history', in their own way are engrossed with this deformation of the growth instinct by an endless hunger.

These are the extreme consequences which have turned upside-down the premises from which we set out. The prolongation of physical growth into psychic maturation and learning, whose increase, in contrast to the physical kind, can always be carried farther toward perfection, experiences things as structurally flawed, never sufficiently developed.

When the Old Testament patriarchs, Eastern sages, or simply the elders of a primitive tribe die, they are physically and spiritually at one, sound and non-neurotic. Getting one's fill of living has nothing to do with taking leave of life. Modern man instead normally dies in despair, because at every age he wants to engorge himself. From an existential point of view, it is cheering to know that even a very old person still wishes to know so many things. They seem to be descendants of Ulysses who draw out through time that need to embark on voyages which the King of Ithaca satisfied in space. But from the viewpoint of the respect for truth, it is dismaying to observe that modern man, who would extend knowledge to infinity, is also the first in history to oblige doctors to hide the truth when they uncover a fatal illness. In finally setting aside Oedipus' quest for truth they join it to Tiresias' reinstatement of the unutterable. The end cannot be named.

---

(31) 'A different Oedipus', Chapter 15 of this book.
(32) In the preceding chapter we discussed how the need of ordinary persons to inquire into origins can take the place of the traditional exigencies of God.

Chapter Eight

Individuation and *Paideía*

An important historical precedent for the concept of individuation is in the idea of *paideía*, which today is often mistakenly understood to have been simply the form of education practiced in ancient Greece. *Paideía*, however, was not limited to the instruction of youth and was based on no fixed programmes. It was conceived as continuing throughout the life of the individual, and as a development of natural, in-born potential. *Paideía* articulated a notion of 'inner culture', or *cultura animi*, which has since receded from Western civilization, with its anti-psychological emphasis on progress, specialization and extraversion, and with its notion that a civilization's 'culture' is primarily defined by its social structures and material tools.

Present-day interest in the Jungian concept of individuation can therefore be seen as a return of the repressed. An analysis of the *Telemachy*—the opening cantos of the *Odyssey*—in which Odysseus' son Telemachus accomplishes his passage to adulthood, reveals the need for a realization of natural potential to be an innate and archetypal ideal. Homeric poetry is then seen to have furnished a unified canon for the whole human being, whereas the subsequent course of European civilization, starting with the Greek Sophists and an ever more specialized notion of philosophy, is seen to have fostered a unilateral mode of maturation. I would argue that nostalgia for *paideía* indirectly reasserts itself through a widespread cultural interest in the idea of individuation.

Introduction

Jungian psychology is indissolubly linked, for better or for worse, with the concept of individuation, which lies, indeed, at its very center. Though Jung repeatedly insists that the notion of individuation is far from equivalent to any defence of individualism, we cannot help but note that irresponsible popularizations have frequently taken it as such. We therefore at times see it pressed into service as a justification for the morally crude and culturally egoistic attitudes of an individualism that forgets to take into account the social bonds and historical ties that no mode of personal behaviour can successfully ignore.

The full worth of the concept of individuation cannot be grasped without constantly reconnecting it to another of Jung's most fundamental perceptions: the collective dimension of the psyche.

Frequently, however, the notion of the collective dimension of the psyche is likewise employed in hasty and schematic ways. We often see it treated as though it consisted exclusively of archetypes, or as though the collective consciousness and collective unconscious were fixed; we see it turned into the notion of an immobile psyche, and thus reduced to a scheme that can be of service only to lazy minds. But psychic life is a process through which we free ourselves from nature and rise above it; such life belongs to the sphere of history and culture, which are anything other than fixed and immobile. If we are to grasp these movements in which the psyche is involved, Jung's notion of the collective dimension of the psyche should be seen as less concerned with the manifestation of invariable archetypes than with an affirmation of the complexity and relativity of the culture in which the individual is inevitably immersed: the culture to which an individual belongs is an indirect presence in his psychic life, and cultures are extremely mobile. Cultural acceptances vary in the interior of any society, no less than in the course of history.

In what follows, I intend to consider individuation less as the subtraction of the individual from her country's momentarily dominant culture, than as a universal (and therefore archetypal, or, more simply, human) need to which various societies and epochs have offered specific possibilities of satisfaction.

The dynamics of a culture should not be seen as working in opposition to the dynamics of individuation. Every process of individuation avails itself of methods and tools which are furnished by the circumambient culture. If we manage to retrieve the true and original meaning of the idea of culture, we will also be able to assert that every culture encourages, to a lesser or greater degree, the individual's tendency to realize personal potential, and thus to effect the process to which we refer as individuation. Indeed, the circumambient culture furnishes the voice and the language through which the individual articulates this process.

In particular, we intend to note that the Greek idea of *paideía*—which today is often inadequately translated as 'education'—hinged primarily on bringing to light the natural potential which is already present in the individual; while taking careful account of the highly significant features that inevitably distinguish a culture of classical antiquity from a modern culture, we will nonetheless see *paideía* as constituting an anticipation of what we now refer to as individuation.

This insight derives its importance from the commonly perceived, and indeed undeniable, fact that the civilization of the modern Western world finds its point of departure in classical Greece. It is of special importance, moreover, for depth psychology, and for Jungian psychology in particular: Jungian psychology sees psychic life as always unfolding beneath the aegis of a myth, and as points of orientation it finds the myths of ancient Greece to be the richest and most meaningful.

An examination of the relationship between individuation and the dominant culture of the modern Western world reveals that history has witnessed an inversion of priorities. The basic flow of culture was once in unison with movements of individuation, but today its principal current runs in the opposite direction. The dominant current of present-day culture is extraverted, quantitative, objectifying and committed to forms of knowledge which are specialized and technological, whereas the development of the interior qualities of the individual has to be grounded on an introverted, qualitative and subjective mode of attention and on viewpoints which are holistic and humanistic.

The Greeks largely accentuated the possibility of individuation, but they did not invent it. Individuation is a basic and natural need which a high culture brings to light and sets into motion, in much the same way that an elevated culture activates our natural need for beauty.

But if individuation is a natural need, we cannot avoid seeing that one of our society's many sufferings centres on the difficulty which this need encounters in coming to expression. A sense of suffering is increased by the fact that, theoretically, the realization of the personal potential of the individual has been recognized as a universal right; indeed the notion of self-realization quite often presents itself as a true and proper fetish. The widespread popularity of analysis in modern Western society, and a particular interest in the Jungian idea of individuation, can therefore be seen as something more than a consequence of an uncontrolled diffusion of the neuroses, of which there was surely no lack in other societies and epochs; it can also be seen as a powerful reaffirmation of the need for self-realization that enjoyed more prospects—despite our so called progress—in ancient Greece than it does in modern society. Perhaps this ancient need is looking for an indirect way to re-establish its primacy, and has therefore opted for the subterfuge of exploiting procedures which are widely accepted by our modern modes of technological and specialist thinking: the procedures of clinical intervention, in the form of psychotherapy.

An analyst is frequently faced with the following situation. A patient undertakes analysis because of some specific symptom, and the analysis then confronts it in the course of the first few months. The symptom (or the group of symptoms) then gradually disappears from certain subjects broached in the sessions. Yet the psychotherapy continues for years. It is not easy to say if the symptom has truly disappeared from the life of the patient, or only from the patient's sphere of interest and from the analytic dialogue. But one easily suspects that the initially presented symptoms were unconsciously accentuated—or even created—for the purpose of having a pretext for finally turning attention to oneself. For entering analysis and cultivating one's own interior life. For the development of one's own particular mode of being.

Interior culture and individuation

Analysts find endless torment in the way their work relates to psychopathology. Analysis was born as a psychic therapy. As an instrument for the treatment of psychopathology, its efficacy has remained limited, especially in relation to the enormous human and financial commitments it involves. It has cured a small number of individual 'discontents' at the cost of great effort and expense.

On the other hand, its cultural influence has been prodigious. From this broader point of view, psychoanalysis has confronted any number of the 'discontents of our civilization' with highly limited means, and at almost zero cost. The thoughts and publications of persons like Freud and Jung have been a true and proper gift to humanity. The discontents of civilization have ceased, ever since, to be the same: they have not been vanquished, but they have surely been transformed.

We have to admit that we do not know whether analysis brings about healing; we can only be sure that it brings about change. But we can also ask if change might not be more important than healing.

Many analysts are far from certain that analysis reduces psychic suffering; but there's a reasonable certainty that it encourages processes through which we become more adult, more responsible, and more conscious. To call such changes 'clinical' is extremely reductive. These analysts look upon maturity as a higher goal than healing; and unlike health, maturity is usually a lasting condition. Maturity can include a healing, or even several, but it transcends healing: it cannot content itself with the elimination of suffering and the restoration of a precedent state of well-being since its tasks are creative rather than normative. Furthermore, if we see our goal within the context of maturity, we have no way of making an a priori decision as to whether suffering is to be combated, or, instead, to be metabolized.

These premises are clearly of concern with regard to any association with analytical psychology, at least in my own country. For a long time, the members of the Italian Jungian associations have continued to prosper whilst showing relative disinterest for the refinement of new clinical techniques, and for the debates, of a medical nature, on their ability to bring about healing. Their activities, in fact, have been evermore thoroughly absorbed by a clientele which is increasingly conscious of the real and concrete expectations with which it makes sense to enter analysis; and this clientele's purpose in turning to a Jungian analyst has less to do with struggling to distance themselves from a symptom than with trying to come closer to themselves. The commitment, in other words, is mainly to what Jungian jargon refers to as the individuation process.

It is not that people who are anxious to deal with symptoms of psychic distress are on the verge of disappearing. But these forms of acute distress are progressively being directed, at least in Italy, to the attention of highly specific forms of problem-oriented psychotherapy, and one notes that the availability of such forms of therapy has vastly increased, and continues to do so. Analysis, on the other hand, is asked to confront the nexus of existential problems. When approached in such general terms, the kind of analysis to which we refer as 'individuative' can ever less be understood as a clinical instrument, and further assumes the characteristics of a form of culture. In doing so, it moves in two directions.

Firstly, it follows a path that starts from the collective and moves toward the individual. The rapid and progressive formation of a global and multi-cultural mode of thinking is witnessing the emergence of a collective consciousness that combines extreme forms of individualism, which typify the West, with models of self-discipline and self-realization that come from the East. In this specific sense, present-day culture (which here is to speak of the culture of so-called 'cultivated' people, rather than of 'mass culture') encourages the individuative mode of analysis.

But it also travels a path that moves in the opposite direction, from the individual toward the collective. For people who have experienced analysis—even if initially with imprecise or traditionally clinical motivations—now constitute a slowly but constantly growing mass of individuals who have discovered 'regeneration'(33) beneath the sign of analytic investigation, who largely enjoy a social and cultural condition that lies above the norm, and who also, in their very own right, exert a powerful influence on cultural tendencies. (It is enough to think of the high percentage of journalists, artists, and writers who have undergone analysis.)

The word 'culture' comes from the Latin *cultura animi*, which is the culture of cultivation of the soul; and the idea of individuation as suggested by Jung (and here it is of little importance that he frequently chose to suggest rather than to define) belongs so thoroughly to the 'proper cultivation' of the interior world as to represent one of its very few forms which today can be propounded. Yet even if it is fully legitimate to see every form of psychological growth on the part of the individual as belonging to the sphere of culture — meaning the culture or cultivation of the soul — we unfortunately have to note that the true meaning of the word 'culture' has been almost hopelessly comprised. 'Culture' is a term which is commonly used in ways that virtually make it coincide with 'civilization', and it can even refer to the tools employed by any given society. This makes it extremely difficult to retrieve its original meaning, and we therefore find it wise to establish a few distinctions.

The original implications of the word 'culture' — as we find them in *cultura animi* — have progressively thoroughly split apart from one another, and we now see culture to consist of aspects which are partly *internal* and partly *external*. It remains quite clear, naturally enough, that every form of culture also finds a seat within the personality. This, precisely, is the problem. As memory turns into an increasingly vast repository of life-support techniques, and as consciousness takes on tasks that range beyond the formation of the individual, becoming more involved with the knowledge that accrues from one generation to the next, culture comes to lie *within* the interior of the individual, but ceases to function as a cultivation of the interior *of* the individual. Such an extraverted notion of culture, which indeed understands it to coincide with the public progress of history, can also be seen as a progressive vilification of the original meaning of *cultura animi*. And many of us now desire to see its return — the return of the culture or cultivation of the soul.

My hypothesis, then, is that the present-day world experiences a diffuse nostalgia for the part of culture to which I refer as internal. To make use of a familiar distinction, we can say that symbols always belong to interior culture, whereas signs find their codification by way of a social consensus that develops in the course of generations and thereby constitutes an impersonal institution that belongs to exterior culture. To give a concrete example, we could also say that there are patients who discuss their dreams without ever learning to interpret them, but who nonetheless allow the analyst to feel that the emotions they encounter in doing so effectively promote their moral and psychological maturation. Others learn quite quickly to interpret their dreams, but we note, as time goes on, that this ability remains unconnected to any process of interior growth. It is clear that the first of these groups of patients is committed to internal culture, and that the second entrusts itself to external culture. Culture comports a real possibility of individuation only for the members of the first group.

Yet the separation of internal from external culture describes a situation that belongs to the modern world, and at the origins of our civilization things stood differently. The Greeks were never forgetful of the meaning and significance of interior culture.

Paideía

The modern world has been described as Hellenocentric, and the numerous considerations that render Greek antiquity absolutely unique, while at the same time being familiar and fundamental for all Europeans, include the fact of its having invented both education and culture, in the elevated sense of the term. Both were implied by the notion of *paideía*.

(The Greeks, however, could never have expressed themselves in such a way. 'Education' and 'culture' are both terms that derive from Latin, and the term *paideía* did not come into use among the Greeks until the age of Pericles, when already it had been at work for centuries and was ready to give its most visible fruits by virtue of having entered the lives of the whole population.)

The novelty of this invention lay first of all in the intuition that the formation and development of the individual was not entrusted to chance or exclusively to the gods: it was also seen to be connected with the individual's 'nature'. The task of the individual was to reach an understanding of his nature. These terms may now seem close to banal, but such a notion of nature was truly a Copernican revolution in a world in which all important events were seen to derive from the super-natural. This, indeed, was the notion that prepared the ground for two of the most salient features of the Western world: its secular frame of mind, and its great consideration for the individual.

I have used the term 'formation', rather than 'education', since history has so thoroughly skewed this latter term towards the external side of culture. We analysts practice one of the very few professions for which the period of apprenticeship demands an interior formation of the psyche—which is our own specific instrument—in addition to the acquisition of external information. The idea of formation is contained in the title of the most important of the texts that have dealt with *paideía*: Werner Jaeger's *Paideia: die Formung des Griechischen Menschen* (34). The secret passion which the founders of depth psychology nourished for Greece certainly was not limited to the myths of Oedipus and Agamemnon; and that passion was even more intense for Jung than it was for Freud. It is no simple coincidence for Jaeger to have written his monumental *Paideia* in the course of the very same period in which Jung was carrying his studies of individuation to their utmost consequences. It is widely recognized that Jung's cultural roots pass back through Burckhardt and Nietzsche into German romanticism, but it has not been sufficiently emphasized that the roots of Jung's concept of individuation do not lie entirely in nineteenth-century romanticism: rather than simply intertwined with the revival of Greek values on the part of the nineteenth century's admirers of the classical world, they indeed pass through it and beyond it and go all the way back to the original Hellenic ideal for the formation of the individual.

Our training, or formation, as Jungian analysts, endows us with a concept of individuation that can serve as an excellent vantage point from which to understand how impoverishing it is to translate *paideía* with terms like 'education' or 'pedagogy'. Just as today we would say of individuation, *paideía* was no simple question of youthful studies; it was a question of the formation of the human individual at all ages. Nor was it limited to the transmission of already classified knowledge; it aimed, quite to the contrary, to understand and develop the qualities whose seeds already lay within the individual: seeds planted by *physis* (nature), but incapable of germination without adequate cultivation (culture).

This notion of a nature that lies within the human individual, in addition to constituting the outside world, was one of the Greeks' most decisive innovations. This utterly secular attitude in the midst of a world inhabited by magical and religious forces was remarkably precocious, and it established a cognitive fulcrum for the subsequent development of all the natural sciences. No other people of antiquity possessed an idea that resembled the Greek notion of *physis*. No other ancient language possesses a similar word. The Greeks admired the Babylonians for their knowledge of the stars, but they were well aware that such knowledge derived from astrological studies on the part of seers who hoped to be able to predict the future, whereas the Greeks' own observations were undertaken in order to grasp the nature of the movements of the heavenly bodies. It was in much the same way that Hippocrates studied the nature of changes that take place in the body and thus founded true medicine as a radically new category of investigation which cannot be considered a refinement of the kind of medicine which already was quite advanced in Egypt.

The observations of nature (*physis*) led the Hellenes to intuit, for the very first time, that its unceasing growth (*physesthai*) derived from a series of rigorous and complex laws for which any sort of divine intervention proved a wholly insufficient explanation. Their traditional divinities had never even been capable of establishing laws that allowed them to live together for more than a day on Olympus without quarrelling. So, how could they have been able to govern the infinite complexity of the world? The Greek gods, moreover, had not created the race of men, and they did not administer human affairs, with justice or providence: so clearly they could not have been responsible for the marvels of the natural world. Faith in the gods rapidly declined and lapsed into superstition not, as is often maintained, with the arrival of Christianity, but with the establishment and affirmation of the concept of nature. This observation allows us to reach a better understanding of the way in which the idea of *physis*, before being refined in the course of the centuries by scientists and philosophers, was a great repository for an infinite variety of values and metaphysical references. It was virtually automatic for the Greeks to endow it with the power to satisfy those needs for universal principles of order which the traditional gods were ever less adequate to embody. Pindar—whose voice, in poetry, can be taken as the synthesis of Greek culture at the moment of its greatest splendour—affirms, for example, that the enormous knowledge which typifies a poet stems from nature (*phya*), whereas a person whose learning derives from difficult studies might, in comparison, be likened to a crow before the eagle of Zeus (*Olympian* 2, 86-8). He exhorts: 'Become what you are by nature!' (*Pythian* 2, 72). He maintains that the superior individual is the person who by nature has true abilities and who makes no effort to acquire them (*Nemean* 3, 40-1). As we hear these ideas, we realize them to hold, at one and the same time, a heroic poetic, an aristocratic code of morals and an archaic version of a naturalistic concept of the world.

Jung's definition of individuation here comes almost necessarily to mind:

> The concept of individuation plays a large role in our psychology. In general, it is the process by which individual beings are formed and differentiated; in particular, it is the development of the psychological *individual* as a being distinct from the general, collective psychology. Individuation, therefore, is a process of *differentiation*, having for its goal the development of the individual personality.
>
> Individuation is a **natural necessity** inasmuch as its prevention by a leveling down to collective standards is injurious to the vital activity of the individual. **Since individuality is a prior psychological and physiological datum, it also expresses itself in psychological ways.** (35)

In the Greek universe, populated by gods who, unlike the God of the Bible, had never known the art of shaping human beings in their own likeness, this metaphysical nature was ready to assume the vacant role of omnipotent being and creator; but also, for the very first time, it left the individual with a space in which it was possible to interact with destiny, rather than passively to submit to it.

Already, as early as the sixth century BCE, when faith in the traditional gods was still quite firm, a critical mind, Xenophanes, had been capable of remarking: 'Truly the gods have not revealed to mortals all things from the beginning; but mortals by long seeking discover what is better' (36). Just as Pindar's convictions seem to be a harbinger of the Jungian ideal of the development of the interior potential of the individual, the growing enthusiasm for the idea of nature, the study of which was hoped to reveal those laws of order which lay beyond the scope of an obsolete religion, is in some ways remarkably similar to the ardour with which early depth psychology greeted the idea of the unconscious. The existence of the unconscious, like the existence of *physis*, escapes direct observation, so even if neither can be banned into the class of fiction, it is clear that neither can be called a certain fact. Yet once hypothesized, classical antiquity's *physis* (an impersonal and invisible entity that lies at the basis of all living things) and modern psychology's unconscious (an impersonal and invisible entity that lies at the basis of all psychic life), both become articles of faith, since they lead to more adequate and comprehensive explanations of a vast array of phenomena in which life as we perceive it is involved.

With all due caution—since caution, clearly, has to be exercised while pointing out similarities between cultural systems that lie at so great a distance from one another—the idea of the unconscious arouses suspicion that it might be a modern example of the same way of perceiving and conceiving new hypotheses that was able to produce the idea of *physis* among the Greeks. Each of these ideas might be thought to represent a specific articulation, suited to the times and society in which it found formulation, of a common archetypal idea. If this is so, the ideal that found expression in Pindar's exhortations, and activation through the practice of *paideía*, would seem to represent the fruit of an ancient system of values that closely resembles the aspirations that today locate their goal in the process of individuation, rather than in healing. The attitude, in both cases, is charged with trust in the powers of nature ('Individuation is a natural necessity...') but aware that inadequately cultivated nature—nature without culture, in the original sense of the term—remains a jungle. To think of individuation as culture—in the light of the original meaning of culture which found expression in *paideía*, and which has since been abandoned by the modern world that conceives of culture in external terms, or as the acquisition of something that lies outside of us and not as a discovery of what one already *is* within one's own interior—is therefore, as suggested at the start, to see it as involved in a cross-fertilization between the cultural situation and the psychic life of the individual.

In the world of archaic Greece, the individual established a place in this cycle of individuation and acculturation—this cycle in which the individual exerts a personal influence on the culture which determines the general parameters of the life which the individual leads—largely by way of *fame*. All the major documents from the era between the age of Homer and the fifth century BCE inform us that fame and glory were the highest Hellenic aspiration. Such ambition had nothing of the frivolous character that a modern mind might attribute to it. Fame for the Greeks was nothing ephemeral—such as the fame to which the modern mass media have accustomed us—for indeed it was quite the opposite. The achievement of fame was tantamount to assuring oneself a place in the memory of future generations. And the memory of future generations, in a society still unacquainted with history, was the only guarantee of any continuity in time: it was the cache that preserved the symbols and values through which the past could give stability to the institutions of the present and the future, and character to the individuals who lived in them.

Moreover, in a world in which religion had nothing to do with any real system of ethics (the ethics implied by the religion of the ancient Greeks at best consisted of a series of prohibitions, but contained no principles that indicated the nature of positive actions), the *example* of the person who had just been rewarded with glory was the single but powerful light that shone through the darkness of a battle against destinies that were nearly inevitable, and with gods who were nearly malign. *So, the only positive form of moral paradigm in the world of the ancient Greeks was extremely explicit, but the examples it offered had to be reconstituted into something entirely new, different and personal.* To follow such an example, one had to supply it with a new incarnation, by means of what we would call a process of individuation. An individual could take a hero for his model; but he knew quite well that he and that hero had different destinies (*moira*), different parents and different gifts of nature. One could use this kind of example as a source of inspiration, but the guiding light it shed had to be employed for the exploration of a new and individual road. So, prior to the era in which philosophy and monotheism began to offer clear and elevated ethical criteria (but also abstract, general and fixed), action in archaic Greece, and also in a part of classical Greece (from about the eighth to the fifth century), was exclusively nourished by narrative accounts of the actions of other men and by individual emotions that such narratives excited in the listener (36). We are dealing here with a heroic ethic that followed no abstract rules; instead, it found articulation by pursuing images of beauty and feelings of glory.

If we attempt for a moment to view this distant society from the point of view that hinges on depth psychology and the notion of individuation, we can feel that the people who were raised in such a culture were not necessarily so different from ourselves, and that perhaps they might have been able to share our concept of individuation to a degree that far surpasses anything that might be found among the more rational minds of later cultures.

We are today convinced that the people of ancient Greece knew very little freedom of action; we see them as living with superstitions, with ever-present magical fears, and with a belief that destiny had already been written. We discover this fatalism in Homer, in the tragedies, and even in Herodotus, whom we nonetheless perceive as the father of the concept of history. We espouse a point of view that oddly disregards the possibility that the absence of clear and abstract rules for identifying good or positive actions, and of institutions empowered to give such rules promulgation (particularly of a religious authority), may in fact have forced the ancient Greeks to live in a terrifying state of total freedom, theoretically much greater than our own; their attitudes of proud solitude and tragic resignation would then represent the place to which they fled for refuge from such overwhelming freedom. We are not to be misled by the existence of religious institutions such as the oracle at Delphi, which indeed was both authoritative and universally recognized. The Delphic oracle pronounced specific replies—which were embedded in cryptic terms—to single, specific questions, and offered no controlling principles or general rules of conduct (if not for the well-known exhortations, 'Know thyself', and 'Nothing too much', which perhaps may have met the needs of a few personalities who already were inclined to introspection and self-discipline, but which surely were too abstract for the populace at large).

The feeling of anguished solitude which surrounded the Greek experience of the problem of morals led to a further exasperation of superstitious attitudes and bolstered the conviction that the gods were untrustworthy, envious and malevolent. But this ethical void, and the terrors and opportunities inherent in such a state of exacerbated freedom, also proved capable of giving birth to *paideía*. *Paideía* was a question of the self-discipline and self-cultivation—and thus, above all, of the interior culture—of the most refined psyche to be found in the world of antiquity. Yet it was nonetheless a psyche that still knew no definition of good or positive actions to which it was proper to direct itself.

In later antiquity, the Sophists often transformed *paideía* into an overly elaborate kind of training (or into an extraverted form of culture), but before that time it was highly essential, and highly similar to the form of growth that takes place in modern analysis. In the absence of universally valid rules, interior maturation was promoted by a profound identification with paradigmatic models, both real and imaginative: maturation stemmed from a search for the individual's own particular myth, as today is still so dear to the Jungian school. These models were the object of a psychic projection, or of a transfer that prolonged and perfected the function of the father; or rather, they substituted the function of the father, since the Hellenic father in fact played a very minor role in the education of his sons. (It goes without saying that we are speaking of masculine *paideía*, since there was virtually no such thing as feminine *paideía*.)

Paideía, of course, was all the more complete when it involved a simultaneous confrontation with an ideal figure (for example, the myth of a hero) and additionally with a real and present model (such as a teacher) that helped a youth to develop an interior image which otherwise might have been too numinous and unapproachable.

Here again, it is interesting to note the resemblance between this ancient process and what Jung describes as 'the fourth stage of therapy' in analysis: after 'confession', 'elucidation', and 'education', this is the stage that sees its goal in 'transformation'. The fourth phase, unlike the preceding three stages, is a process of growth and development in which the results cannot be known at departure, but only on arrival. Another difference between this stage and the others lies in its requiring something more than the technical participation of the guiding figure: it hinges on the whole of that figure's personality. In a psychotherapy that does not limit itself to dealing with symptoms (or to so-called 'support'), and which directs its efforts, instead, to individuation, we find much the same state of affairs that we encounter with the figure of the hero with whom the Greek youth interacted while modeling his adult personality: Jung remarks, speaking of such a situation, that 'the personalities of doctor and patient are often infinitely more important for the outcome of the treatment than what the doctor says and thinks' (37).

Telemachus: the maturation of a depressed young man

One of the best known examples of *paideía* is contained in the first four books of the *Odyssey*. They apparently centre on the search for Odysseus on the part of his son, Telemachus, but their real theme is the young man's rapid interior growth. (Many scholars, in fact, refer to these cantos as the *Telemachy* and treat them as constituting an independent work which only later was incorporated into the *Odyssey*.)

At the start of the story, Telemachus is highly embittered, owing to his knowledge of the way in which his mother's suitors are, little by little, depriving him of his house, his throne and his future. However, his only response to their arrogance is silence and passivity. We are told that 'in his heart, he fantasizes his glorious father' (I.115) who might return at any moment and vanquish the evil-doers. But we are not to forget that his father had been away for all of twenty years, and that Telemachus is unacquainted with him. So, *Telemachus is not cultivating a memory, but conducting an interior dialogue with an ideal ego for the purpose of shoring up his own.* Active imagination, as a form of spiritual gymnastics for the reinforcement of psychic growth, is no recent discovery.

Rather than the boy's father, a noble foreigner by the name of Mentes now appears, presenting himself as a friend of Odysseus and claiming to have been united to Laertes—Odysseus' father and Telemachus' grandfather—by ancient ties of hospitality. Mentes, however, is the goddess Athena in disguise. (We are not to be led astray by the fact that a male *paideía* is guided by a female divinity: Athena is the divinity who, more than any other, 'belongs only to the father' [Aeschylus, *Eumenides* 739].) She is so thoroughly enmeshed in the 'father complex' as to have been born from Zeus alone, unaided by any mother.)

The unexpected guest offers his assistance to Telemachus and serves as a bridge that helps him reach the guiding image which is to preside over the path that leads to his maturation. (Though nominally the image of the father, this figure that appears in his fantasies is in fact an ideal image, and as such is the 'child' of his own imagination.) Mentes' association with Laertes, Odysseus' father, alludes to the possibility that Telemachus' maturation as an individual may in fact preserve his link with all of his various ancestors. In his conversations with Telemachus, Mentes finally predicts the return of Odysseus; but we should note that this prediction is a separate and almost auxiliary affirmation. What Mentes announces has less to do with the reappearance of the real father than with the entry of symbolic energies and activities into the life of Telemachus. When asked for a definition of his qualities—an indispensable premise for every process of growth and differentiation—Telemachus confesses an anxious lack of confidence in himself as an adult, since he lacks all identification with the father and is still constrained to turn to his mother for spiritual nourishment, like an infant who is not yet ready to be weaned: 'My mother calls me his son, but of that I have no knowledge of my own. No one, alone, can know the seed from which he springs' (I.215). Telemachus here complains of having no direct relationship with anything paternal, insisting that even the knowledge of having a father comes to him by way of his mother.

Telemachus states quite clearly (I.231-45) that his predicament lies less in the absence of his father than in the arrest inflicted on his growth by the fact of having lost contact with the image of his father. For Telemachus, the presumed death of Odysseus is first of all an interior event; it is the emblem of the way his own soul languishes on the plant of life. This condition is itself more painful than the knowledge that his father is dead. The death of a father who has died a glorious death that then carries his name on everyone's lips, and consequently to immortality, endows a son with a life and an identity. Odysseus, on the other hand, has simply disappeared in the course of his endless voyages, perhaps destroyed by the Harpies (here understood as goddesses of storms and tempestuous winds) who were known to capture still-living men and drag them down into the world of the shades. As though by osmosis with his archetypal father, the identity of Telemachus seems likewise to have disappeared in the course of endless mental voyages, the wanderings of his childish fantasies. Like the physical life of the father, the psychic life of the son seems to have been overwhelmed by destructive feminine forces: storms of the soul that constitute his own interior Harpies.

The example of Orestes (mentioned by Mentes at I.300 and by Nestor at II.300) also hovers in the air around Telemachus' *paideía*. Orestes was the son of Agamemnon, and in addition to his father's name, he also inherited his father's violent death, and then had gone on to ensure immortal fame for himself by vindicating that death and re-establishing justice. Fame became his reward for an extreme form of courage. By raising his hand not only to kill Aegisthus, the assassin, but also to kill his own mother, Clytemnestra, who had been Aegisthus' accomplice, Orestes had waged a solitary battle against the most terrifying monsters of his own interior life. He proves himself capable of victory not only over the enemy, but over himself as well.

Mentes, or the patriarchal wisdom figure who assumes that disguise, counsels Odysseus' son and offers him a number of points of advice: the council of the people of Ithaca will have to be convened, and its summoning will mark the first occasion on which Telemachus assumes his identity as the king's heir, for since the time of Odysseus' departure twenty years previously, the council has never again been called together. Telemachus, moreover, is to issue a warning to the arrogant suitors: in symbolic terms, the disorder they represent is not to remain unbridled, and Telemachus is to start to interiorize and exercise the authority which he cannot forever project onto the image of the unknown father. He is also to exercise his authority over his mother, Penelope, by sending her away to King Icarius, her father and his grandfather, therefore severing the umbilical cord which keeps him immobilized in his own past, and which taints him with a quality, a touch of something feminine, that does not befit him. Penelope confronts a dramatic problem: is she to remarry or not? On the counsel of Mentes, the problem of 'the mother' has to be contained by 'the father', and decided by the father. Penelope has to regress, returning to her original condition as the daughter of Icarius, and allowing the decision on a new marriage to be left up to him (I.275-787). And, finally, Telemachus is to outfit a ship and depart in search of his father.

Odysseus' son listens spellbound to Mentes' words, finding them increasingly convincing. He then remarks: 'You have spoken like a friend; indeed like a father to a son' (I.307-8).

Homer's poem presents us with the situation in which Telemachus suddenly (and for the very first time) removes himself from his mother's authority. We have to remember that a mother, unlike the father, remained eternally a minor for the ancient Greeks. We observe him as he searches for information about his father, we watch him prepare his voyage while he does so in secret, informing no one at all, not even his mother. We also note that this course of action is inspired by prudence and a sense of responsibility: Telemachus has to be careful to raise no alarm among the suitors. So, it is truly a question of achieving the ability, for the very first time, of making a decision, and of suffering the anguish of moral solitude while doing so; it has nothing to do with a subterfuge on the part of a disobedient son. Homer remains entirely unaware of any such base motivations and actions; the images through which he speaks are always noble. He knew that he was a teacher, and he understood the nature of such a task. Even the ruses he attributes to Odysseus are always cunning and creative, and never in any way sinful: they mark a dawning of intelligence, rather than any eclipse of morality. Just as the poem leads Telemachus to maturity by putting him in touch with a series of elevated metaphors, the story that recounts his development itself becomes a metaphor that elevates the soul of the listener by the force of its own example.

Telemachus's companion on his voyage is again the goddess Athena, who once more assumes the guise of an older friend. The name she uses this time has since served as a synonym for a guide and counselor: Mentor (38).

Mentor encourages Telemachus to continue to pursue his path, since he is convinced that the young man's interior already holds the acorn that can grow into an oak. He remarks (in paraphrase): 'If you are not the son of Odysseus and Penelope, you will not accomplish what you propose to do. But if you are, have no fear of feeling fear. You will not be able to be cowardly or foolish' (II.270-75). His nature as an individual already exists; now he has to allow it to grow; he has to cultivate it.

At their first stop, Telemachus and Mentor encounter Nestor, the oldest and most respected of the kings who gathered at Troy. Telemachus grows bashful and stands at the verge of allowing himself to lapse into total passivity. He does not know what to say or how to behave, and he confesses his perplexity to his older companion: 'But Mentor, how am I to approach him? How am I to greet him? I have no knowledge of such things...' (III.22-4). Mentor, however, shows Telemachus the nature of his responsibilities, saying that the knowledge of how to approach such a wise and authoritative king cannot derive from any external suggestion, and has to spring from interior feelings: 'Telemachus, some thought will arise in your soul, a *daimon* will give you an inspiration' (III.25-7). Unlike our current forms of education, but quite in line with our understanding of individuation, Telemachus' *paideía* cannot proceed on the basis of fixed norms that are equally valid for everyone. His progress depends entirely on the development of his own potential; and such potential, like a *daimon*, lives invisibly within the personality of the individual.

When Nestor inquires about the purpose of the visit, the young man's reply concerns symbolic rather than material intentions: he wants to reinforce his own identity, and he already knows that this is his principal need. So, instead of saying, 'I am looking for my father', he answers, 'I am looking for the great fame of my father' (III.83). At the next stop on his voyage, at the court of Menelaus, King of Sparta, he again states that he is not looking for his father, but for his father's fame (IV.329). Rather than tracking down a man, Telemachus is pursuing the traces of an archetype. This single phrase contains many of the themes we have already discussed: paradigmatic examples as the seat of moral principles; the search for fame as an affirmation of individuality, and not at all in acquiescence to convention; and interior dialogue with an ideal image.

We know now that Telemachus' voyage is symbolic: the sea through which it cuts is freedom; the ship on which he sails is experience; and along the way, he is not to encounter his father, but to discover adulthood.

The loss of Homeric unity

The elevation of the material, as briefly remarked above, is a constant and essential feature of the Homeric poems.

Epic is a thoroughly aristocratic genre, and this is seen in its psychology even more than in the social class with which it deals. Everything in Homer is noble and beautiful: laughter no less than tears; the succulent foods and the wine that warms the heart; the precious gold and the gleaming bronze that deals out death; the generous word and, additionally, the clever ruse. Nothing is futile, crude or base since everything stands in the service of a higher purpose.

This also applies to the *Iliad*, even if the morals it supplies are crueler and more primitive than those of the *Odyssey*. Achilles' stubborn ire is never a gratuitous vulgarity, but instead is a state of unconsciousness that soon will lead to its opposite; it is a vagary that summons the realization of a proper destiny. Achilles' ire is a necessary tool for holding Agamemnon's arrogance in check; and, above all else, it is a necessary factor in his own maturation. The pain Achilles experiences when his friend Patroclus is slain by Hector is in turn the necessary experience that allows him to abandon his haughty caprice and forget the quarrel with Agamemnon which has spurred him in refusing to do further battle. Now he can return to combat and render elementary justice to Patrocles by defeating and killing Hector. The death of Hector then reveals its full significance in enabling Achilles to know the pain of Priam and to abandon another form of excessive pride. Finally, the whole of this chain of sufferings is the indispensable prelude to the next and already predicted death: the death of Achilles himself. Having matured in the course of these many events, he is fully aware of his destiny and hastens to encounter it. He accepts the principle of universal justice which decrees that no one can hold first place for too long a period of time; he knows that precisely the strongest die at the earliest age.

This archaic tale does not ring strange to the ears of a Jungian analyst. It describes a path that inevitably leads the individual to become what his or her very own nature and destiny require, with nature and destiny here to be understood as a kind of unconscious intention on the part of the personality.

The teleological slant of the tale is something else that makes us find it familiar: we recognize this world in which evil is never entirely evil, since its final goal is growth and transformation. The exploration of mechanisms that support this process fill them with the power of a guiding light: we witness the defeat of modes of thought that nourish themselves on suspicion, or of the prejudiced sets of presuppositions that insist on the predominance of evil. Such thinking muddles a great deal of literature, and as well a great deal of psychology. We find Homer's evil familiar because it lies outside the sphere of cause and effect, and refuses as well to be reduced to a question of pathology. As a teleological evil, it serves a purpose: it conducts the individual to the heroic solution of overcoming a situation that allows no other exit.

Though we speak of Homer, we cannot be sure if we are speaking of one, two, or any number of persons. Indeed, we may owe the *Iliad* and the *Odyssey* to a large number of authors. But the cultural unity of the Homeric epics lies beyond question. They give us a recapitulation of archaic Greece, and indeed lend nobility to the whole of Hellenic antiquity, since the following epochs continued to see them as their most antique and fundamental myth. No other epic, no matter the height of its purposes, succeeds in speaking quite as simply of the human being, rather than of some specific society and of some specific type of human being, most usually of the warrior. It is enough to consider the humanity which the *Iliad* attributes to the enemy, in the person of Hector (whose feelings and actions are presented, at times, as even more elevated than those of the Greeks), and then to compare it with the crude picture offered by the Chanson de Roland of the Saracens, presenting them always as unredeemably evil.

No other literature so suddenly began with two works of such completeness and complexity. The infancy of few other literatures is marked by masterpieces: this achievement on the part of ancient Greece is another measure of its greatness. Homer contains everything, and in seamless, still uncorrupted unity: history and myth; the gods and men; matter and spirit; ethics and aesthetics. The *Iliad* and *Odyssey* were the books that spoke the truth, and at the same time the compendium that held all books. Such a seething plethora of images may perhaps have induced a sense of confusion and solitude in the listener. To listen to a man who sang the verses of the *Iliad* and the *Odyssey* while plucking the strings of a zither-like instrument (they were composed, we must remember, for precisely this purpose, and certainly not for reading) was a concentration, within a single collective rite, of just about everything which might today be an evening of culture, a social event, a recital of music or poetry, an appeal to patriotism, a sermon, and a religious ceremony. The listeners' commotion must have been enormous. Whilst learning the achievements of august models that had lived in an indeterminate past, they knew themselves to be living in different circumstances and could capture no more than the energy of certain emotions, finding inspiration but no clear directives for their own most proper courses of action. Beneath the brunt of such stimulations, these listeners most likely had no other choice than to resign themselves to destiny, or to grant wholehearted acceptance to that acceleration of maturation which today we refer to as the individuation process.

Epic was the force, both chronologically and culturally, which set off the whole colossal process of progressive accumulation that led to the modern world, of which our every idea or gesture is the progeny, and to which Homer quite surely never turned a thought.

Herodotus, 'the inventor of history', asserted that the forms and genealogies of the gods, along with their many names and attributes, came exclusively from Homer and Hesiod: it was already clear that Homer had done something more than simply narrate a fable, and indeed had given codification to the whole Greek faith (39).

Plato was so thoroughly convinced that Homer had been 'the educator of Hellas' as to find it deeply disturbing: the ideal state that his theories constructed—abstract thinking was itself a major Greek invention of the post-Homeric era—could contemplate no possible place for all the sentimentality and irrationality of epic: 'Homer is the greatest of poets and first of tragedy writers; but we remain firm in our conviction that hymns to the gods and praises of famous men are the only poetry which ought to be admitted to our State. For if you go beyond this and allow the honeyed muse to enter either in epic or lyric verse, not law and reason, which by common consent have ever been deemed the best, but pleasure and pain will be the rulers in our State' (40).

Fortunately, millennia later, we can say that Homer has defeated Plato. He has proved to be the better prophet. He holds that stature by virtue of having concerned himself with the whole human being who acts first of all on the basis of profound emotions, and not only of rational thought.

So, already in ancient Greece, the work of Homer not only exerted enormous influence at a popular level, but the author also stood at the centre of the debates among creative minds. Its birth marks the origins of a creative process which has never drawn to a close.

In the era preceding the Homeric epics, culture had moved by starts and stops. The so-called Hellenic dark ages (from about the twelfth to the ninth century) had cancelled out the achievements and barely preserved the memory of splendid civilizations, such as the Mycenaean, which formerly had trodden the same soil: its fortresses were still solid, but no one knew who had built them, or for whom; and the meaning of its writing, which no longer could be read, had been lost. The Greeks had regressed from palaces to huts, and from a written to oral civilization.

But the beginning, more or less, of the eighth century BCE witnessed the start of the process that turns Western culture into a cumulative culture which has ever since continued, up to the present day, to amass and preserve its achievements. (Compared to the Hellenic dark ages, Europe's dark or middle ages were a far more limited regression, since European culture did not abate, but emigrated and resided among the Arabs for the space of a few centuries.) Remembering that most scholars indicate the eighth century BCE as the epoch in which the Homeric poems assumed their final form, we can conclude that their author (or authors) took vigorous part, beyond all conscious intent, in an immense *paideía* that saw the formation of everything of cultural relevance which appeared in the following centuries. Homer fertilized the ground on which the whole of Greek culture was to flower—or we could say that he played the role of an archaic group therapist—and this explains the poems' ability, even today, to reveal its essence, despite dating from its start, and not from its final phases. Even Plato, who was basically critical of Homer, saw him as the fount of Greek tragedy (Republic 595ff.). Further proof of the way in which Homer goes hand-in-hand with the affirmation of a new mode of human existence that displays a constant interest in the development of the psychic potential of the individual can also be found in a highly important historical coincidence. Another of the innovations from the eighth century BCE lies in the birth of the two institutions which ever since have represented Greek ideals of the body and the soul: Olympia, where physical life sought its maximum expression in victory in the Olympic Games, and Delphi, where the spirit appealed to the oracle as the highest source of truth. It can also be added that this period more or less coincides with the appearance of the Greek alphabet, which is still employed today, and which constituted the basis for all European alphabets. Remembering that Western culture, throughout the course of its history, has always cast a backward glance at ancient Greece whenever it has hungered for ideals, we must recognize these years as having marked a definitive watershed. If seen as a cultural rather than religious continuum, the West, indeed, might begin its time-line with Homer rather than Christ.

This, then, is the point that interests us. The centuries immediately following Homer already showed great advances in every field; yet nothing was so grandly complete as things had been before. Not even the Greek tragedians surpass Homer's works, which they drew upon for inspiration. Post-Homeric Greece can perhaps be said already to have witnessed the inception of what we consider a modern evil—the evil of specialization—and in spite of the mammoth conquests of the centuries that followed Homer, no form of culture continued to be able to address itself to the growth of the whole individual.

Homer still presents a unified model of the human being: ethical and aesthetic, in war and in peace, both for Greeks and non-Greeks (who, significantly enough, were not yet called 'barbarians'). We would see this fact quite clearly whilst reading his poems, if we were not so encumbered by habits of reductivism. Some modern commentators have freely remarked that the Homer of the *Iliad*, who recounts a war, understood very little of military techniques, since whilst describing the engagements of densely packed armies he always ended up by isolating and describing individual duels. They note that, yes, his heroes reach the scene on chariots of war, properly driven by charioteers, but that then he makes them descend and sends them into combat on foot. This is no proof at all that the author was ignorant of military tactics. Homer was first of all interested in the valorous single actor, the model individual; and the glorification of such individuals was the primary purpose to which he bent his every scene. He knew the tale of Achilles to hold a unique moral power as an instrument of *paideía* (even if 'moral' and *paideía* were words that did not yet exist). He sang of the individual model; he therefore insisted on man-to-man duels only; he paid no attention to horses or charioteers, so as to keep them from absorbing a part of the action; he wanted nothing to distract our gaze from the pure individual.

Greek lyric poetry, appearing in the seventh and sixth centuries BCE, constitutes the invention of a highly precocious form of introspection, and would indeed be a complete proto-psychology if not for the fact that it dwells almost exclusively on the movements of the inner life. Philosophy made its début in the fifth century BCE, shattering the unity of the high Homeric ideal (the man of *kalokagathía*—valorous and beautiful) by insisting that the mind is superior to the body. This attitude, for example, made aristocrats and important citizens no longer to feel it was their duty to take part in the Olympic Games; at most they furnished the horses which were ridden by others. So the Olympics ceased to be a total rite, or religious, cultural and physical at one and the same time. We here find the start of the specializations and fragmentations that lead to the kinds of soulless (and often mindless) sports, reduced to simple bodily exercise, that we know today. Philosophy's disruption of the unity of the individual was also a question of supplying the individual with ethics that were separate from and superior to aesthetics. Philosophy takes no account of the powerful emotions that accompany the experience of the beautiful; it presumes instead to furnish stable, rational knowledge of the good.

Homer's tales are charged with emotion and excitement and had inspired their listeners to identify with the great heroes; Plato's truths, on the other hand, could only take hold in theoretical thought, or in those who place their lot in the primacy of the mind over the body, of ethics over aesthetics, and of intellect over profound emotion—which is clearly a one-sided attitude for anyone concerned with psychology.

We recognize the Greece—and above all the Athens—of the fifth and fourth centuries BCE to have held the greatest and most flourishing concentration of artistic and intellectual production that history has ever known. We tend, however, to be less aware of strictly related parallel developments that may even, in historical terms, be unique: in the space of only a century, starting with the staggering victories over the Persians and the explosion of the Athenian enlightenment, *paideía* spread throughout the whole society and became the regulating principle of the lives of all: an astounding cultural revolution. Life was no longer controlled by royal commandments, by gods, or by any other outside force, but only by the need to develop one's own nature.

We can allude only briefly (41) to the way in which this highly particular society was eventually pushed to an ego inflation by these sudden achievements, and may even have reversed, by *enantiodromia*, its formerly typical attitudes. These were its dignified resignation to destiny; its fear of excessive well-being and intelligence (since great distinction could attract the envy of the gods); and the sense of terror which traditionally had taken the place of a system of moral principles, which, as already pointed out, was lacking in Greek society. Greek civilization was to turn, almost suddenly, into something it had never been before: into the basis, through its discovery of quantitative thinking, of the expansionist policies of European civilization. On making the acquaintance of monotheism, that civilization would ally itself with God, replaced in the modern age by science, and effectively assert its hegemony over all other world-views.

Conclusion

It is widely known and accepted that the *polis*, or the city-state, was one of the greatest of the many cultural innovations that the Greeks brought into existence. Rather than a body of citizens who came together for purposes of defence, commerce, or for any other practicality, the *polis*, with its participatory, grass-roots democracy, and its sudden and rational secularism, its uninterrupted vivacity of invention, is something, moreover, that cannot be explained as a simple result of the extension of democratic rights to the whole of the populace. Such things can be decreed swiftly, even today, without making even the slightest dent in a situation of spiritual poverty. The novelty of the *polis* lay in its rapid generalization of the ideal of *paideía*.

Up until the golden age of classical Greece, *paideía* was still the culture of the soul in the most genuine sense; and the unrivalled flowering that derived from it might be explained—if we find any pleasure in paradoxical affirmations—as the first and only mass individuation known to the course of history (if 'mass' is a term that can apply to the thirty or forty thousand male citizens of the city of Athens). Or it might be called history's only mass aristocracy (considering that the controlling ideal of this male elite had remained the Homeric ideal of aristocratic *areté*, which translates as 'virtue' or 'excellence').

It is clear, however, that this happy combination of quality with quantity could not last; and, in addition to this, it never again was to repeat itself. An elevated level of median culture, drawing upon some of the institutions and thinkers which *paideía* had fostered, was destined to endure for centuries, but it ceased to be the culture of the soul. It lapsed into specialization and came to be offered in the form of pre-established techniques, without any further encouragement of the aspiration to grasp and develop one's own unique and particular talents. The Sophists, particularly, marked the inception of a new class of cultural adepts who also served a new market. Since they couldn't satisfy everyone, they turned to those who most insistently demanded their attentions, creating a new *de facto* elite which knew nothing of nobility. The development of the learnable skills of the self no longer had anything to do with becoming what one is by nature. So, in spite of the continuing emergence of large numbers of intellectuals, the masses of the people at large soon began to feel the frustration of this cultural loss; they could not keep up with the pace that the Sophists and their students set, and their loss of the Homeric ideals was already definitive. At the same time, the democratic institution of the *polis* began to dissipate and finally disappeared beneath a flood of quarrelsome policies, which additionally were often base and invariably destructive, ushering in various types of tyranny and oligarchy.

Greek notions of quality therefore grew ready to be overwhelmed by Roman commitments to quantity; and even more importantly, from our own point of view, the ideal of the complete man was definitively supplanted by the ideal of the specialist who directs his attention to immediate and particular goals, such as those that still today remain our principal concerns.

If I have been taking the liberty of comparing individuation and *paideía*—while well aware of the risks, the overstatements, and the limitations that such a comparison entails, especially within the brief space of an article—it has not been solely for the purpose of arguing that the idea of individuation has an ancient and noble ancestry. I also feel that in developing our understanding of individuation, it is worth our while to discuss the psychology of *paideía* in itself, and to appeal as much as possible to its original meaning, since it still has a great deal to teach us. As we reconstruct the atmosphere that typified the lives of our Greek forebears, the ideal that promotes the realization of the natural potential of the individual begins to present itself as an archetypal ideal.

From this perspective, it is easier to argue that our culture's loss of *paideía* has induced a vacuum that sooner or later had to be filled with the Jungian idea of individuation, or with other forms of acculturative consciousness (such as the Oriental philosophies) that could serve as its equivalents. The fact that analysis began its life as a clinical instrument might even be seen as incidental, since it was necessary for analysis sooner or later to take the turn toward a path of individuation, as Jung in fact was the first to propose for it.

It is not necessary to adopt so extreme a point of view to find reason for alarm in the possibility that the emphasis on clinical specialization—now increasingly encouraged by the laws that are starting to regulate psychotherapy as a clinical discipline—may lead analysis to lose its potential as a unifying force within culture, as a route that fosters the growth of the whole and conscious individual. If individuative analysis finds its precedent in Greek *paideía*, the excessive specialization of psychotherapy, if allowed to take its place, may well end up by consigning analysis to the fate to which the Sophists consigned *paideía*: its transformation into a rapid course of specialized development for which the final price is a gradual disappearance of the original and fundamental ideal.

First published in English, translated by Henry Martin, in *Journal of Analytical Psychology*, 1997, vol. 42, pp. 481-505.

(33) Many can be said to have been 'converted' rather than healed, as already has been remarked by Lévi-Strauss; see *Structural Anthropology* (1958). Allen Lane/Penguin, London 1968, chapter IX, p. 183.
(34) Werner Jaeger (1936). English translation by Gilbert Highet, *Paideia: The Ideals of Greek Culture*. Oxford University Press, New York, 1943-44.
(35) C.G. Jung, 'Definitions', in *Psychological Types* (1921), *Collected Works*, vol. 6. Princeton University Press, Princeton, 1971, par. 757-8 (bold type added).
(36) Hermann Diels, *Die Fragmente der Vorsokratiker*. Berlin, Kranz, 1951-2, fragment B18.
(37) Hans-Georg Gadamer, 'Das Vaterbild im griechischen Denken', in H. Tellenbach, ed., *Das Vaterbild in Mythos und Geschichte*. Kohlhammer, Stuttgart, 1976, p. 106. (See also Gadamer, *Gesammelte Werke* Band 6, chapter 13. Tubingen, Mohr, 1985. Not yet translated into English.)
(38) Both 'Mentes' and 'Mentor' contain the root *men*, which means 'constancy' or 'perseverance'. This is one of the qualities that Telemachus had to develop.
(39) Herodotus, *The Histories* II, 53.
(40) Plato, *Republic* X.607.
(41) This historical reconstruction has been presented at length in my *Growth and Guilt*. Routledge, London, 1995.

Chapter Nine

Destruction and Creation

We are growing tired of hearing only about "creativity". The repetition of this term represents creativity as if it were only one more article of mass consumption. Ever since our thinking has been challenged by Jung's, we have come to suspect that such a view is one-sided, and we look instead for totality. We suspect such a view of being exclusively of the light and seek to fill it out with shadow.

In this sense we can say that the psyche wishes not only to create but also to destroy. The unity of creation and destruction strikes one forcibly in Italy. According to estimates by UNESCO, the Italian peninsula has more than one quarter of the world's art treasures: 100,000 churches, 40,000 castles and fortresses, 3,500 museums, etc. Nature and humankind alike take care to crown this immense work of creation with acts of destruction. Italy is a country of volcanoes and landslides. Forty-five per cent of its surface is exposed to the hazard of seismic shocks, including the earthquakes recorded in recent years which have swallowed up the artistic treasures of central Italy.

Human beings also play their part. Despite enormous advances in cataloguing and conservation, around 35,000 objects vanish each year from Italian collections and museums, or about 100 per day. The passion for loveliness also murders it. Venice is sinking not only beneath the sea; a city of fewer than 69,000, it is now flooded annually by more than 15,000,000 tourists.

Yet can we be certain that malicious nature (floods, earthquakes, and volcanoes, the destructive shadow of the creative earth mother) and mankind the sacker of cities (the dark plundering shadow of its luminous inventive drive) are always enemies of creativity because they no longer sustain life? In reality, the volcanic eruptions on Thera (Santorini) and at Vesuvius have both assaulted and saved immense quantities of Minoan and Roman artifacts that would have been lost forever, erased by time and human egoism. Human beings in fact have always tried to eradicate all signs of the cultures that have preceded them, if these differ from them in the slightest. Only most recently with regard to human history, only in the last two centuries, has the unbridled curiosity of Westerners systematically begun to collect such traces. Hence major European colonial powers have snatched up great treasures from Mediterranean Europe and other continents. Yet it is difficult to ascertain just where their actions have been negative or affirmative. Plunder may have reduced life to something that survived because it was mislaid. Looting may have been a destructive act—the final humiliation of a conquered country—yet at the same time creative, the beginning of an absolute respect for art, for creativity as such. Creative intentions can never escape a destructive shadow. But destructive intentions carry a creative shadow. Nothing has depth without its own contrary.

Let us now step back and consider the birth of a work of art. The destructive act is not only something that can follow creation to preserve it. It can also be the initial condition, the originating move that frees the creative act.

Behind the Renaissance discussion of the differences between painting and sculpture, something much less specialized is at work: a universal and timeless depth, of maximum interest for Platonic thinking and for Jung's psychology. Benedetto Varchi had raised the problem of the nobility of the arts among different artists. It is well known that Michelangelo, the master of every means of expression, preferred sculpture. Writing to Varchi from Rome in 1549, Michelangelo did not simply declare that preference but went on to distinguish among the forms of sculpture. The truest sculptor does not work with clay, for that way of making sculpture at bottom resembles painting, dealing with the laying on of a substance (colour or clay, regardless) and lending it form. That way is rather limited because it is not a complete, vital process: it does not add *and take away*, create *and destroy*. True sculpture, says Michelangelo, 'works through its powers of removal'.

Removing, rejecting, eliminating: to destroy the natural surplus within the marble block. Creation is not accumulative but reductive. Man does not have to make or install a form that is already part of things. Man need not produce an idea; he need only free it from an irrelevant weight of stone.

In that sense, for example, the 'Prisoners' are among Michelangelo's most representative works. While they portray captives as their subject, at the same time they render the fact that every sculpture by Michelangelo is imprisoned in a marble mass. *Creating* a sculpture meant *destroying* its place of confinement.

In looking at a block of marble, Michelangelo tried to *see* this confined, ideal form. The artist is someone who attacks the block with chisel, discards excess matter, breaks the chains which bind the form and shatters the useless stone.

We may imagine the sculptor smashing away with superhuman force and then, once his idea has burst out, stopping, exhausted by his own aggression. That gives some impression of the 'unfinished' style of the 'Prisoners' and of Michelangelo's sculpture as a whole. The work is not smoothly dressed, but jammed among slabs of the half-worked block. Its power and movement derive from exactly this fact, showing not only the prisoner who wishes to break out of jail but also the idea that wishes to emerge from the material and go untrammeled the moment it does so, still struggling to shatter the crust of marble which strangles it. Such sculpture is not a static and polished product but the image of this struggle.

Nor is it, in psychological terms, the achievement of a human ego, but of an archetype that wants to take form, and in doing so has enlisted the ego in freeing it from the dross of a motionless and inorganic condition. Consequently, centuries before Jung, Michelangelo has proven the existence of the archetype and of the fact that the artist's task is not proudly to create it but to sense it, intuit it, to perceive it and free it from the primordial sleep which has enveloped it in the bowels of the stone.

Accordingly, immersed in a Platonism which for him was not the philosophy of the schools but the truth of life, a Renaissance master employed 'the unfinished style' to serve an inner exigency, centuries before modern expressive conventions took a similar path with less vitality.

The chisel of Michelangelo may stand as a metaphor of the analytic commitment. From an individual and clinical point of view, Jungian analysis does not seek to 'heal' the 'illness' of patients so much as to help throw off the waste stone that incarcerates them, to destroy the psychic calcification, the impersonal stoniness that cloaks the true and individual form of each being. Which is to say, to retrieve the harmonic sustained by the archetype beneath the crust of daily presumptions: an ever-present value which nonetheless calls for destruction-creation to set it free.

But the Jungian analyst also carries a cultural responsibility. Today, when one hears that gangs of youths have taken to smashing works of art, one cannot be content with calling the police. One must ask why the chisel of Michelangelo—in which destruction and creation are one—has been forgotten for hundreds of years, why it has slipped so far beyond reach and why only the barbarians have thought to drag it from its slumbers.

A slightly different version of this essay appears in English, translated by Elizabeth Teefy, as an introductory talk in *Florence 1998—Destruction and Creation: Personal and Cultural Transformations. Proceedings of the Fourteenth International Congress for Analytical Psychology, Florence 1998*, ed. Mary Ann Mattoon. Einsiedeln, Daimon Verlag, 1999, pp. 13-16.

Part Three
The Classics Up–To–Date

Chapter Ten

Homer and Mass Communications

Let us talk about one form of mass communication by way of symbols, leaving abstract concepts to one side. Let us turn to images, and how myth-making employs them, but also how a modern mass medium does the same thing. We need not call upon the thought of either McLuhan or Baudrillard. Think of a still more famous writer, simpler and more original. Let us return to the starting-point of European history and European literature, to the roots of our imaginable world and the grandfather of all writers. Returning to origins means returning to Homer, and therefore to his first poem—the *Iliad*—in a few of its initial scenes.

Before making our way into the *Iliad* we must, however, take a detour in order to conjure something of the atmosphere that came with the classic heroes. Ancient epic and tragedy, unlike modern literature, sacred scriptures and in general all the other texts that we are familiar with, do not speak of moral wrongs or describe individual pettiness. Epic is in every way aristocratic. Instead of evil there is wretchedness, instead of unjust actions there is destiny. Everyone carries out his task, even as destroyer and bringer of death, in an elevated style and a noble manner. Hector slaughters Patroclus, not cruelly but with something like melancholy, because destiny appoints him as the conveyor of irresistible sorrow to Achilles; because in that way Achilles will renounce his wrath and again enter the lists against the Trojans; and so Hector's destiny will culminate in his slaying by Achilles, but then immediately Achilles himself will die, squaring his accounts, too, with destiny. It goes on in this fashion. Patroclus, Hector and Achilles, friends or enemies, all will meet death nobly, with a smile or a tight-lipped phrase, noiselessly.

Achilles is indefatigable in killing Trojans. Nevertheless, when his corpse begins to redden the waters of the Scamander, the river god is offended and punishes it. In turn, Greek tragedy deals with horrendous crimes, and yet, as everyone will recall, observes an unwritten law; it does not put death on view, it never spills blood on stage. As for sexuality, all forms of it were permitted and practiced without inhibition in ancient Greece, yet epic as much as tragedy makes only the briefest, most indirect allusions to them. Blood and semen may flow into rivers, but with a soft gurgle, noiselessly.

In ancient Greece there was no distinction, as there is with us, between good and bad taste. This happens for a very simply reason: bad taste is unthinkable, or does not exist as a mental possibility. Heroes can be tragic but not malicious, homicidal but never vulgar. When finally one of his characters behaves with obvious dishonesty, Homer does not show it as such, but as an intervention by a god who has swindled the man. From this viewpoint, his mightiest heroes sustain an almost infantile ingenuousness.

Yet it would be a mistake to think that Homer's serenely noble style reveals an archaic or somehow limited ingenuity. Homer certainly was no infantile mind describing a Kindergarten world. On the contrary, the Homeric mind knows that cynicism, egoism, utilitarianism and an altogether histrionic shallowness dominate human passions. He shows this with programmatic clarity in the initial episode that we are going to rehearse. But it is one thing to be conscious, under no illusions, that baseness lives in this world. It is quite another thing to let it drive a realistic description of the world. In his second canto Homer allows himself to dramatize cynicism for one second, only to cudgel it irreparably with the sceptre of kings and heroes.

His unfenced wisdom, like that of a great philosopher or saint, therefore extends itself to the full reach of his time and the world it describes. Homer's rather antique verse knows how to speak about evils which also belong to us. It also in fact addresses the irreconcilable opposition between the heroic world that prefers elevated, noble literature, and the lazy world that gives itself to mass communication.

Agamemnon has offended Achilles, who, indignant, will no longer fight the Trojans. Inspired by an evil dream from Zeus, Agamemnon not only will not change his mind, but conceives an ingenuously omnipotent scheme. He thinks he can launch the final assault against Troy without Achilles' help and conquer it without sharing the glory, even though Achilles has long been the strongest of the Greek allies. Yet Agamemnon's arrogance does not stop there. Before sounding the attack, he wants to put the bellicosity of his troops to the test. He gives a speech in which he professes his discouragement, saying that he has given up on taking Troy. Naturally he waits for the army's obligatory spasm of pride and unanimous shouts of 'No! We'll push on to the end'! Instead they respond with a cry that modern Italians have come to know very well: 'Strike the tents, launch the ships and hoist sail! Head for home'! In a flash all is chaos. From one line to the next the Greek host evaporates. The *Iliad* itself crumples beneath our eyes and disappears. In a trice a maddened horde of insects stampede through the camp, throwing their gear helter-skelter into the ships.

We witness here the first moment of epic poetry's sudden slide into mass communication, signaled by this down-slope tumble of imagery. The heroes have vanished, giving way to a crowd ready to flood into every cranny, but not to choose. Only the eloquence of Ulysses can still persuade the runaways to fall back into line; the moment he speaks, he begins to restore order. However, it is too late. Epic verse goes to pieces. Heroic bardic song has routed itself. The hour of Thersites has struck: the very soul of the despicable, the man whom one cannot name. We have reached the second moment in the eruptive advent of mass communication: after the great images become all-too-human comes the voice that floods into every cranny—unlike the heroic voice, it lacks resolve and is without purpose.

Thersites is an anonymous figure without compare anywhere in Homer, but to whom, contravening every epic convention, he grants full freedom of speech, thereby lending a voice to every base instinct and creating a distinct counterpoint to the speech of heroes (in this case the commander-in-chief Agamemnon, and Ulysses who deepens his own dialectic in the attempt to restore order). With Thersites Homer has lowered from heaven—or better, has raised from hell—an antihero on the plains of Troy. Thersites is already all there at first glance: lame, stooped and bald, a shabby and cowardly rascal like Nietzsche's 'last man'. In the place of intelligence he has cunning. In the place of dignity he cultivates interests, and for honour he substitutes advantage. Thersites ought to be only one Greek soldier among many, but he seems above all to be a symbolic figure, an emblem and distillation of the craven spirit that explodes in the Greek camp. Throwing away the book, the basic primer of Greek epic, the *Iliad* puts Thersites on stage without naming his father or city of origin: a unique kind of treatment in Homer, which goes a long way towards speaking for his character. Yet more singular still is the gash that opens, every ten lines or so, in the fabric of epic.

The *Iliad* becomes no longer a poem, but instead shifts into something else, more like a TV talk show. There are no breaks or dead spots, for when Thersites opens his mouth quantity takes the place of quality, exploiting every chance to be heard, even at the cost of provoking extremes, boredom or annoyance. And utterly without poetic or heroic themes, which demand an attentive ear and, in the hearer, a noble attention corresponding to the speaker's own. It is much easier to spread gossip and slander about the powerful: the effort required is minimal, whether from the speaker or listener, while envy and the baser instincts ensure a large and amused audience.

Thersites—the *Iliad* tells us—spoke without intermission, shapelessly. He was clever, knowing many expressions by heart, but without command and with no genuine purpose he used them to speak ill of kings and heroic commanders; he was in fact convinced that this was the way to entertain the Achaeans. He was hateful above all to Achilles and Ulysses, whom he ran down at every turn. But this time he flung himself with his sharp tongue against Agamemnon. Thersites knew very well that the Achaeans despised their commander, but silently, in their hearts. Therefore it was easy to get their attention by hounding him in full cry.

> *Still moaning and groaning, mighty Atrides—why now?*
> *What are you panting after now? Your shelters packed*
> *with the lion's share of bronze, plenty of women too,*
> *crowding your lodges. Best of the lot, the beauties*
> *we hand you first, whenever we take some stronghold.*
> *Or still more gold you're wanting? More ransom a son*
> *of the stallion-breaking Trojans might just fetch from Troy?—*
> *though I or another hero drags him back in chains . . . .*
> *Or a young woman, is it—to spread and couple,*
> *to bed down for yourself apart from all the troops?*

(The original Greek at this point uses vulgar expressions, unusual in Homer. Here the author has leapt from epic poetry into mass communication, having shown with surprising foresight how easy it is to 'build an audience' by deploying a bit of pornography.)

> *How shameful for you, the high and mighty commander,*
> *to lead the sons of Achaea into bloody slaughter!*
>   . . .
>   *Home we go in our ships!*
> *Abandon him here in Troy to wallow in all his prizes—*
> *he'll see if the likes of us have propped him up or not.*

> *Look, now it's Achilles, a greater man he disgraces....*
>
> (II.211-240, tr. Robert Fagles)

Homer therefore has suddenly made visible not only the elevated but also the ignoble, by fashioning a vessel for incessant, slanderous, vulgar and defeatist blather. To put it in modern terms, he has set pure entertainment against poetry. In doing so, however, he has sealed the vessel and thrown away the key. The antihero and entertainer will stay locked inside, while the open spaces are restored to the hero and poet.

Ulysses intervenes at this point:

> *What a flood of abuse, Thersites! Even for you,*
> *fluent and flowing as you are. Keep quiet.*
> *Who are you to wrangle with kings, you alone?*
> *No one, I say—no one alive less soldierly than you,*
> *none in the ranks that came to Troy with Agamemnon.*
> *So stop your babbling, mouthing the names of kings,*
> *flinging indecencies in their teeth, your eyes*
> *peeled for a chance to cut and run for home.*
> *We can have no idea, no clear idea at all*
> *how the long campaign will end . . .*
> *whether Achaea's sons will make it home unharmed*
> *or slink back in disgrace.*
>
> (Book II.246ff. tr. Fagles)

Therefore, Ulysses argues, the Greeks should put an end to all useless talk and its attendant distress, and stop pretending that they are stronger than destiny, which accomplishes its ends without consulting the opinions of mortals.

Let us notice here how the hero's speech even becomes the opposite of mass communication. Today it is necessary to talk about wars because they make us anxious; this anxiety generates curiosity about war, because fear makes news. The excuse for talking about it, for satisfying the voyeurism of death in the living room, is pretending that mass information really allows one to know more: to know beforehand what the war's end will be and of course to affect the outcome.

Ulysses concludes his rebuke with a cutting assessment of Thersites's 'ranting slander' and its devious ability to gain a hearing from the disaffected and war-weary troops, and then a promise to thrash him if he spouts such material again, 'to grab you, strip the clothing off you, / cloak, tunic and rags that wrap your private parts,/ and whip you howling naked back to the fast ships,/ out of the armies' muster — whip you like a cur'! With that Ulysses grabs Thersites and pummels him on the back and shoulders with Agamemnon's studded golden sceptre. Thersites, crumpling beneath these blows, suddenly falls silent, his tears drying as he squats on the ground. The Greeks rally again, heartily approving of Ulysses's firm canniness. Furthermore, the nameless fighters finally abandon their indecision: the temptation towards base cowardice had spoken within them as well, through the symbolic mouth of Thersites. In order to return to a nobler motive, says Homer, one must silence babbling and gossip. One can achieve this only by way of an indisputably higher authority, an impress represented by the king's gold sceptre.

Certainly, to see in Thersites simply the coward contrasted with heroes does not exhaust the meanings of this scene. That view does no justice to the complex world which one can intuit while standing on the *Iliad*'s shoulders, a world in which only the dukes and the warriors count, while a miserable rabble are probably compelled to trail after them reluctantly on the road to glory, where they have no choice but to idolize, envy and perhaps silently hate them. From the viewpoint of social criticism, Thersites is the voice of their courage. Many recent commentators on Homer plainly emphasize this point. But is it a case of reading Homer as a social text, or a text in the psychology of the anonymous mass? Neither, I believe. Many modern texts can tell us more about such things. What makes Homer unique, all over again, is something else: he tells us that the first forms of mass communication show up in a far-off time, directly in the *Iliad*. Additionally he shows that these forms of mass communication rise in direct opposition to the spirit of heroism. From this point of view, Thersites is an extraordinary forerunner, a true prophet of the vile.

With one stroke Homer cleaves through heroic epic and, down a 3,000-year-long fissure through the eras, he at last sees us. Looking, he describes the world of television and the illustrated magazine. He sounds this out in a contemporary voice, rather familiar to us: 'What are you up to now'! He joins to this a rampant and pseudo-political theme about the end of both peasant civilization and of ideals: 'You have the right to refuse, to think of your own particular interests'.

This tone is more important than how many seem to give ear to Therisites, for it reveals a highly unusual Homer. Therisites does not don Greek armour, but the sweat-stained jerkin of drudgery; he yells no war cries but hollers 'The water's boiling'! In characterizing him, Homer has rendered no classical hero but a character out of Alberto Sordi, anticipating the paradoxical popular entertainment in which caricature lets one mock one's own vices, cowardice and egotism. Through a ritual of apparent criticism, one gets used to treating these failings as normal and therefore benevolent.

This last bit of conditioning, however, is a recent development. Homer would have no part of it. How different we are from the figures of ancient epic, living in a world that calls whatever happens on TV *real* and whatever does not happen there not only *unreal* but non-existent. Such is the reason for paying attention to anyone these days. So why study Homer any more? Even we, peering down that long crack through the eras, sometimes catch sight of the bard himself, but only to yell, 'Homer! Keep Achilles, keep Ulysses, but give us Thersites'!

Chapter Eleven

The Helmet of Hector

A few days ago, beginning a book by Peter Handke, I came across this sentence in the first chapter: '*Hinter dem Glas wurde ihm nicht eine 'tochter' entgegengehalten, oder gar ein 'Nachkomme', sondern ein Kind*'. (What appeared behind the window was not a 'daughter', certainly not a 'descendent', but a child.) (42)

In the second chapter comes a sudden recollection while he watches the girl on a carousel: 'Then a scene from his own childhood came to the man, in which, though he found himself in the same room, he had heard his heartsick mother crying aloud: are not that woman and myself, both of us now here, one and the same? I now see the figure on the merry-go-round, rising and falling while she turns, as the counterpart of a grown-up, appearing for the first time as an autonomous figure, independent of the parents beside her; and I see that I must give more power to this freedom. The space separating the two figures stretches out triumphantly and the man looking is himself the little figure on horseback in a tableau, behind which strongly now sounds the play of waters from the piazza" (43).

If Handke is thought to be one of our major contemporary writers, it is due not only to his skills of psychological description but also to the themes which he treats. Central among these is childhood, as metaphorical as it is real. In addition, one of his principal books is dedicated to his daughter's first years of life. In it, through an innovation he chooses as much through narrative as through essay writing, the Austrian novelist has spoken of the father-daughter relationship, described a father-daughter family, and narrated the father's typical condition from the father's side. It is paradoxical that we must inquire into the fact that Handke's originality derives from a theme which appears to be rather old and shopworn.

The father's condition does not go back to the gradual differentiation out of original symbiosis, such as from the mother-child relation which the author remembers. Nor from anything else. It simply arrives ready-made. Even if the commonplace is false, that in the animal realm every 'father' is limited to fertilizing the egg and plays no further role in raising the young (among many species of birds these tasks are divided equally between father and mother), it is undoubtedly true among the larger animals. Ethology and anthropology draw the same conclusion, that the human father function—which has him organize the family and provide for its needs—is an invention of civilization, and therefore the invention of fatherhood substantially corresponds to the invention of the family, and accordingly to the initial phase of civilization.

In this sense the father is probably in on the beginning of everything, and therefore in no trivial way positions himself at the origin point, and in the centre, of the great trope of monotheism. Before the father, most likely, there was society but no family. Before the father there was prehistory but probably no civilized order worth recording. And yet as civilization undertakes gigantic advances, and does not become extinct, laboriously starting over from scratch with each new generation, this giant preserves its feet of clay down the centuries. Such a potent invention could only combine with an omnipotent psychology which secretly negates its own artificiality and is shot through with a permanent precariousness. To the mythic aspects of this vulnerable omnipotence we shall return shortly.

'The evidence suggests', writes Margaret Mead, 'that we should phrase the matter differently for men and women—that men have to learn to want to provide for others, and this behaviour, being learnt, is fragile and can disappear rather easily under social conditions that no longer teach it effectively. Women may be said to be mothers unless they are taught to deny their child-bearing qualities' (44).

In this sense the invention of the father is not only the job of civilization but also a task of Sisyphus.

The contrary thesis, though part of a rather complicated argument, is relatively simple. If the force of the paternal role is the decisive element in the development of civilization, the strongest societies and groups will have a strong father, and vice versa. It will suffice to consider American society for a moment, with its strong patriarchal propensities among the Protestant and Jewish sectors, and the unhealthy marginalizing of the African-American underclass, for the most part made up of families ruled by a mother or grandmother. Exactly as Mead has argued, with slavery the father fell into oblivion because rights could no longer be recognized nor duties be taught, while the maternal world survived intact. Mothers could not be sold without children, but fathers could. Therefore the backbone of the black family came to be broken through the course of centuries.

Since we are concerned with the relation between myths and reality, it is necessary to draw keen attention to a false myth that is spreading through Western culture at the moment: that the past one hundred years have witnessed a universal decline of the father. It is true that the traditional family and its patriarchal hierarchy have been placed on the defensive in recent decades by the explosion of mass media and horizontal communications—for example between young people the same age—which challenge both conclusiveness and verticality. On the one hand, however, it is also true that the modern era began not with television but, according to several points of view, with the Renaissance or the discovery of America, in any case exactly at those times and places in which the typical bourgeois family began to assert itself in the modern Western world, and which in various ways continues to reinforce itself up to very recent times. On the other hand, the decay of the patrocentric vision (not to be confused with the authority of single fathers within families) already sets in with the spread of Christianity which, over against the absolute Hebraic Father and the absolute authority of the Roman *paterfamilias*, lends authoritative voice for he first time to the Son. Things therefore are considerably more complex than popular opinion would have us believe.

It so happens that not only does the image of God stand for the father, as Freud claimed, but also that the father stands for God and a complete metaphysical system into the bargain, if one, by affirming grandeur or decadence, constructs tales about historical appearances and metaphysical substantiality. The more that false myths shape the understanding of the father the more they can take advantage of genuine mythical figures, with outlines that simply parade their essential attributes of strength versus weakness.

No single image will ever be vast enough, yet some can go deeper than others, being better able to take us to the roots and the heart of the problem, namely to Greek civilization. There the chronological and cultural tree of the West first grew, marking the noblest yet most extreme phase of the West's patriarchal propensity (so much so that modern European languages still call homeland 'patria', which in Greek means 'earth of the fathers'). The Greeks also take us to the work of Homer, which remains their Bible.

In contrast to all other literature that we customarily call heroic, the Homeric poems present, with descriptive precision, the father's role: Odysseus' with Telemachus in the *Odyssey* and Hector's with Astyanax in the *Iliad*. Let us close with the description of Hector, which in one respect is extremely simple, and in another, by general critical agreement, affords the fullest and most poetic figure; a view which justifies the supposition that he was Homer's favourite too.

Analogously to what we find in many modern novelists, Homer's description of the father-son relation, even though he speaks in the third person, substantially views matters from the father's side. As with Handke, and just as Mead confirms in her study of primitive peoples by relating fathers across cultures and millennia, the relationship with Hector's son is not a given. The infant Astyanax remains perfectly trusting in the arms of his nurse and his mother (*Iliad* VI.467, 482), but when his father wants to lift him he pulls back, frightened. Unlike the contact which the boy has with a woman, the one with Hector does not originate with his birth. It is not a natural encounter, but is conversely mediated by cultural forms. Obviously Homer composes not with modern-day terms, but with the images that were meaningful in his own time, and which are more convincing to us than our contemporary concepts. So, in fact, a man looms before the child as a tremendous, menacing god, encased in bronze armour and a towering helmet with tossing horse's mane (VI.469-70).

The parents smile. Hector removes his helmet, and at that point can kiss the boy and take him in his arms. He lifts him high, uttering a prayer to Zeus that one day this son may be mightier than his father. How remote from our modern shabbiness, including what we have tried to unload on the Greeks, calling it the Oedipus complex, which construes the primary bond between father and son as a two-way envy!

We have said that the father is civilization's giant with feet of clay, its foundational institution, omnipotent yet secretly fragile because, unlike the mother's role, it undergoes continual recreation with each generation and in every individual. Every institution that is truly new, every cultural structure that is at once revolutionary and newborn, distinguishes itself as all-powerful, rigid, fanatical and aggressive. To compensate and even face down this precarious condition of its own, it props it up with guillotine and armaments, with the elimination of enemies and doubt. Thus the father down through today is compared with the mother. Which is not to say, therefore, that the masculine, which we know zoologically to be more aggressive (though that is not always the case), is to be compared with the feminine. Rather it is precisely the cultural institution of the father that we know to be in need of armour—as it knows itself to be—in order to survive.

That is because men—fathers and not men in general—invented laws, the state and armies. This last grouping is probably a cultural prolongation not of punishments but of a defense linked to the anguish of non-existence: as we know, even among lions, punishment is reserved to the male, although killing falls to females. Aggression in the human father is no natural condition. On the contrary, it expresses the terror of returning to that condition. If the mother in a given culture loses her own proper authority, she nonetheless continues to be a mother. If a father loses his, he loses the sense of his own being.

Let us therefore again take up my point in asserting that if in every society fathers stand apart from mothers through authoritarianism and aggression, then that difference is not the consequence of an instinct, which already distinguishes masculinity among animals as a combative tendency, but of a role acquired over time from the specifically anxious-making condition in which they are billeted at the core of civilization; a condition over which they do not necessarily rejoice and which often, like the helmet of Hector, pointlessly frightens the sons.

Hector's helmet does not point to that fact alone. It also shows that a father can understand the fear inspired in his son by his gleaming weapons, can then smile and, doffing his breastplate, embrace him very much as would his mother.

Homer's wisdom does not end there, however. It lays out that tragic alternative to which history, steaming our way through blood, seems to have given itself. Hector is in fact the only complete hero in Homer, capable of shifting when necessary into the sensibility of home and hearth, which is wrongfully described as feminine in the same way that women prejudicially construe work as masculine.

Nevertheless the killing of Hector at the hands of Achilles is the culminating event of the *Iliad*, which says a great deal about the mythic patterns to which Greece chose to entrust itself, the society whose stories, layered through the centuries, make up Homeric epic.

Achilles is in fact Hector's antithesis. He too plays the father, yet we know nothing about his relation to his son, except for learning that he too becomes a warrior (*Odyssey* XI.510ff.). If Hector is the strength that holds up the family, Achilles is the axe that topples it. Hector's wife Andromache urgently reminds Hector how Achilles exterminated her own family, killing her father and seven brothers (*Iliad* VI.414ff.). If Hector is the voice that tries to contain such destruction by subjecting warfare to a chivalric code, Achilles is the berserker who takes fighting back to the jungle. At the climactic moment in his duel with the Trojan hero, Achilles rejects any laws of war, or rules of engagement, throwing away the book for that blood we believe animals drink because no contractual terms are set up 'between men and lions, wolves and lambs' (*Iliad* XXII.261ff.).

It appears at this juncture that Homer's tale, like prophetic intuition, has grasped what was destined to prevail among the two mythic patterns which he sets out. It would seem that he has announced beforehand the defeat of the more complete one in favour of the one that is weaker within families but stronger in public, political and military spheres. It would also seem that in this way he has prefigured across millennia the gradual ascendancy of an institutional power which fails to correspond in the same degree to the differentiation of affections (and sufferings, by implication) in the private realm. Furthermore his intuition precedes us down to the recent past, in which the great paternal tropes driving affairs of state have devolved into a competition distinguished by tyranny and plunder, indirectly compelling the patriarchal family to take the same downward path, and at last join in a vicious circle with those public and private forces intent on discrediting the father across the board, on social, familial and intrapsychic grounds.

Before resigning ourselves to this prospect, we might ask ourselves if Hector must necessarily succumb when he goes out to face Achilles.

A talk given in French to the SFPA (French Society of Analytical Psychology) in Paris, 1999.

(42) Peter Handke, *Kindergeschichte* (1981). Suhrkamp, Frankfurt am Main, 1984, p. 11.
(43) *Ibid.*, p. 25.
(44) Margaret Mead, *Male and Female, A Study of the Sexes in a Changing World*. Morrow, New York, 1949, p.192.

Chapter Twelve

The Soul of Midas

Nature tends always to fullness of variation and to satiety. Animals in the forest feed themselves and mate, but they do not indulge in orgy and gluttony, for their appetite shortly settles down. The forest itself is quickly satisfied with an equilibrium in which everything has its place. Trees grow neither endlessly nor too densely. Their wings shield the understorey, which in turn leaves the earth to grasses which give way to mosses and such, as long as space is filled but not overcrowded with signs of diversity. Only modern man has invented monocultures—vegetative metastasis—where completeness is thwarted as much as possible; where only numbers multiply while variety goes altogether absent; where plants choke themselves out and infect each other. Man too has invented the city, the monoculture of the human animal, which piles up until it cries, 'How crowded, how awful to see nothing but cement'!

It used to be that profuse wealth meant beauty because it was also variety. Not by accident, treasures in antiquity consisted of precious stones or jewelry: jewels as joys (*gioelli: gioie*), a feast for the eyes, an infinitely varied spectacle. Today wealth is an ever lengthening and ever increasing bank statement, or a wall of offices utterly the same but assessed at millions per square metre.

The psyche (*anima* or soul) is that most intricate part of the human being for which natural laws cannot wholly account. It has no stomach to fill and its hunger is infinite. The psyche or soul has had to become the new dimension of humanity, a meta-zoological one. This dimension is the dwelling place of knowledge, art and religion, everything that raises it above the animals. When it falls into neglect as a zone of inner activity, it unconsciously invests in the outer world as projection, as the need to feel reaffirmed by unlimited wealth and at the same time to reassert our superiority over the beasts, the dominion of our 'anima' over the bodies of 'animals'. The animal—which our language has designated in that way because it also attributes to it a soul or anima—must become purely a possession, in fact entering into the systematic bookkeeping of our belongings. Consequently today's expression 'pecuniary worth' means 'value expressly as money, in accounting units'. Originally, however, pecuniary indicated 'expressly in *pecus*', as heads of livestock. 'Capital' has the same etymology from heads of stock. All of this thus far from Latin; the English *fee* in turn comes from French *fehu* (cf. the Italian 'agave il fio') or 'livestock'. This is identical to the original meaning of German *Schatz* (treasure), from the Germanic root *skatta* (livestock). The Greek obol comes from *obelós*, a piece butchered from animal sacrifice.

This is enough to remind us that originally wealth was a living thing, in fact an animal, supplied therefore by the anima. Originally soul and wealth did not simply face each other in contradiction; on the contrary, they were absolutely continuous.

The psyche has had a way of gradually differentiating itself from our animal aspect, inventing new ways of being such as laughing and crying, things not so much contrary as complementary. The chief creative expression of antiquity, the theatre, staged comedy and tragedy together in series. Dramatic representation gave—as opposed to modern practice—equal importance to wisdom and mystery: to learning and ignorance, to teaching and silence. In sum, to having contraries coexist. Mystery cults were at the same time dark and joyous, transmitting a certain kind of knowledge yet strictly prohibiting ever making it known. Nothing could claim to be absolutely good; the relativity of values and the complementarities of opposites were thoroughly acknowledged. Far off indeed lay our delirious representations of radically unilateral matters such as *the happy ending* and *the happy few*.

Being exclusively happy was inconceivable or, worse, something that was avoided out of superstition. Being rich led to the same outcome because it was shown as one-sided. Not that gold was despised, but neither was scarcity greatly prized. They knew instinctively, and codified in myth, what economic science formulated only many centuries later, in more tedious, skimpy and fundamentally less convincing terms: that if wealth is made up of uniform elements and too widely circulated it thereby brings on through inflation the very poverty it was meant to eliminate. In summation: if a good thing becomes too common it turns bad.

Today we seem to divide ourselves into immoralists who sell the soul for cash and moralists who see cash as the guillotine of the soul. Yet the badness is not in things themselves, which change according to how they are used, but in this amputated one-sidedness. Wealth and money are not originally the irreconcilable opposite of the soul, but rather its complements, one of its protections against the outer world. In antiquity, gifts of money came to persons made virtuous by heroism or wisdom, because their worth and their irreproachable proof against the corruption of the time symbolized their inner qualities and extended them to the outside world.

Polycrates ('many-gifted'), the lord of Samos, is described by Herodotus as an altogether worthy tyrant blessed by the gods. But his good fortune is too great; he has been too successful in heaping up wealth. His good friend the Egyptian king Amasis wrote to him with concern: 'Substantial riches are an adornment, but too much wealth is arrogance, insupportable to the gods, an incitement to their jealousy. Quickly divest yourself of what is most dear to you and return to right measure'. Sailing far out to sea, Polycrates then threw his costliest ring into the depths.

Shortly afterwards, however, a fisherman paid homage to him with a large fish, which was found to have swallowed the ring. Destiny, then, did not will him to become rich in the moral or complete sense, in which one knows abundance and poverty together. Polycrates subsequently let himself be tempted to reach after still greater wealth that would have made him lord of the Greek archipelago, but fell into a trap and was crucified. Polycrates, a slave to riches, died in a manner unworthy of free men and reserved for slaves (*The Histories* III, 39-126 *passim*).

Let me repeat for the sake of clarity: originally wealth was not the enemy of the soul but one of its external expressions. Mankind is close to God in monotheism and in polytheism to a primordial wisdom; both of these proximities make the good things of life an extension of things metaphysical. The secular notion of wealth did not yet exist.

In the Earthly Paradise mankind has no knowledge of luxuries. The same goes for Hesiod's myth of the Golden Age. Nevertheless, already with the apple of *Genesis* human beings discover an appetite for things unknown to animals. And so, ages before any clinician began talking about pathology, bulimia came to be. Ages before the invention of economics we had inflation, because taking hold of whatever lies over and above necessity harms the one who possesses it. Long before becoming a technical slippage in economics, inflation was a moral fault.

Dionysus was a vagabond. Let us remind ourselves how pertinent his personality is to our argument. More than any other ancient god, Bacchus presides over the integration of differing qualities, from discord to uniform accumulation; he stands for the universality that resists one-sided or unilateral qualifications. He stands apart from other Greek gods because he was worshipped everywhere without distinction, his cult not being tied to any one region. In contrast to the strictly masculine or feminine attributes of the other gods, his sexuality was ambiguous. In contrast to the most distinctive quality embodied in the other

Olympians, he managed a mode of being which in our eyes is contrary, but which for the ancients was complementary: wisdom and drunkenness. Finally, his cult in large part was a mystery religion, observed publicly while being maintained with the utmost secrecy.

The god had his customary retinue of satyrs. Here a modern voice might ask, 'How can Dionysus represent balance, a universal poised against the particular, a harmony of complementary needs, when he is surrounded by satyrs, who are the emblem of insatiable sexuality'? This voice, however, has already gone off the road, confusing modern pornography—utterly one-sided—with the complexity of classical *eros*. In reality we are far from an adequate understanding of the satyrs, precisely because they are tied to many aspects of the mysteries. Among the few things we know for certain, however, is the fact that their name has the same meaning as the word '*saturo*', or 'satiated', precisely the opposite of an uncontrollable appetite. Therefore along with the satyr's erect phallus in permanent sexual excitement goes its opposite—once again, so to speak, not a single, one-sided attribute but two extremes in equilibrium.

In this retinue one remarks a notable absence: Silenus, who was lost, swaying beneath years and too much wine. Midas will find him again.

Ancient sileni ran in packs, much as the satyrs did, with one exception: Silenus the preceptor of Dionysus. This figure is impossible to analyse. Silenus practices wild behaviour and makes love like a young man but experiences things like an old man; he is both reckless and prudent. Silenus teaches and, ever on the road, learns anew. Silenus gets drunk as a sage does, wise and sloshed together. He is crowned with garlands among which the loveliest gifts of nature weave themselves, yet that same nature wryly equips him with a ludicrous potbelly, leaving him both handsome and gross. The apparently contradictory complexity of Dionysus is exalted in his master, pushed to an extreme. Correspondingly, antiquity thrusts its knowledge down into the greatest depths. The highest praise that Plato will give to Socrates compares him to Silenus (*Symposium* 216d). According to Aristotle, Silenus was robbed so as to make off with that incomparable endowment. Compelled by Midas to speak, Silenus reluctantly said that as for human beings it were better had they never been born; if they do enter this world, it is best that they die right off. (See also Pindar, fragment 157, where Silenus retorts, 'Miserable creature of a day, your boasts about money are babble'.) Imparting knowledge is all very well. To communicate the depths of wisdom, however, inspires flight because it is horrendous. I believe that it is no casual bond of kinship that links the name *Silenus* and the word *silentium*.

Let us turn to the tale by Ovid. The vagrant Silenus was discovered in the fields at harvest time by certain peasants, who led him to King Midas. They recognized the old man and rejoiced, for to them he was the embodiment of profoundly moving ritual practices. In fact Midas, according to legend, had been personally initiated into the Orphic cult. After a lengthy celebration of this discovery, Midas brought Silenus once again to his young pupil, the god Dionysus. The god in turn was so overjoyed at this reunion that he promised Midas the satisfaction of a wish, whatever it might be. Then came the unfortunate request, 'Make everything I touch turn to gold'. In itself, the wish for gold was not enough to shatter the metaphysical order of the world into which it intruded itself. Midas's world knew nothing of banking, and gold was not exclusively a unit of accumulation as such. Gold was the symbol of divinity, immortality and kingship. Yet such 'allness' is suspect and leads to ruin: how can one always and only acquire gold? One-sidedness inhabits this trope. It is too much to ask of fate; it can only end badly, even if not in the manner of Polycrates. Then there is the list of useless treasures: no food, because it turns to gold when the tongue touches it; no water, for the same reason; when weariness makes one lie down, the mattress is steely; and so on. In the end the king persuaded the god to free him once more to his 'sumptuous poverty'.

Dionysus will grant the quest, and Midas will have to plunge into the Pactolus River and climb it all the way upstream to its source; in doing so he will free himself, one step at a time, from the accursed metal. Gold, according to one of the conventions of civilization the thing of greatest value, annulled the king's ability to satisfy his simplest needs: eating, drinking, sleeping. Yet without these animal functions this civilization and all its riches perish. In order to save them it is necessary to withstand the onrushing torrent of human invention, and to move in opposition to its tendency to leave its own source far behind. The power to go against the mainstream current is indeed necessary, without, however, going all the way back to the point at which that inventive flood spurts from the earth, where attaining it is simply a continuation of nature.

Midas can breathe his own air again, because he has returned to the human sequence of gain and loss. From the viewpoint of modern economics, he has discovered the essential distinctions between exchange values and use values. But from a psychological point of view he has taught himself something more. In effect, Midas had exchanged Silenus for gold. He had bartered away the nocturnal complexity of values in the mysteries for the manifest, clear and gleaming values of precious metals *tout court*. Additionally, he had renounced the depths of wisdom inherent in tragedy and the mysteries, for the calculable positivist value chased after by the fickle crowd. The many do not uniquely represent the psychic poverty of those who wish only to get rich, but in a more general way, they are fixated on seeking an exclusive value in wealth, thereby forgetting that according to the myth it vanishes into thin air if it is not plunged into complexity and chained to its own opposite.

Chapter Thirteen

The Rape of Europa

The disturbing novelty of the 21st century is not the construction of a new territorial expanse—continental and multinational—powerful as never before in history. It is not even the fact that this union is laced together by floods of money rather than by rivers of blood. The real novelty, quite unprecedented, is that this titanic event is taking place silently, in the absence of myths, rituals and symbols.

In reality, a myth of Europe exists, but it is as if that myth belongs to the past and not to the future: to 'others' and not to us. For Europeans, the inhabitants of a European country that is not theirs will always remain as for 'the others'.

What we are saying is that the European distinguishes himself not in belonging to the country in which he lives, but precisely by not belonging to it. The European speaks with infinite adjectives and with infinite, ambivalent feelings. Yet when he exclaims, 'that *great* country, America', he speaks with open admiration bordering on envy. Yet no European wants to belong to a great country. Perhaps such a country means great responsibility; and history, always bearing down heavily on Europeans, accustoms them to thinking and feeling in small terms.

Still, even in ages past, there existed something that we call Europe. Greek myths speak of happenings in maiden Europe, and by the time of the first written history, from Herodotus, a geographical entity called Europe already exists. And throughout the history of the West the typical character of the region takes shape. Therefore, lending it definition should not be too difficult. The defining characteristic of Europe indeed ought to be definite rather than confused, and its identity therefore clear.

Europe exists as unity within strength; the idea itself of the strong state is European. At the same time Europe is extremely diverse and pluralistic; in no other place in the world has such a multiform culture concentrated itself within such a confined space. The idea of the nation state, too, is European. The national state was not invented for geographic or economic or dynastic reasons but because of extant ethnic diversity.

Early on, group definition derived from being either part of a tribe and its kinship ties or from standing subject to a ruler to whom a shared allegiance was due. Much later it became logical for a group to assume a common definition if it shared the same language or religion or territory. But to Europe and its nations this rule is rather difficult to apply.

Blood ties by this time enter in minimally, even if the word 'nation' should refer to origins (Latin *nascor, natus*; cf. Italian *nascita*) which are shared in common. The United States have taken to calling themselves a nation along European lines, but its people are immigrants, born in widely different places. Nor does allegiance to a sovereign enter in; the French remain French when they obey their monarch or, in times past, after they have cut off his head. At the heart of Europe rests Switzerland, a confederation of micro-national entities, a European experiment in miniature which has survived happily for seven centuries, therefore longer than the nation states. (It is true that France or Austria are still older, but for a long time they were ethnically and linguistically diverse, and thereby nationally plural.) Belonging to Switzerland is certainly not given by way of linguistic or religious unity. Nor does it come even from living there, seeing that Swiss citizenship maintains itself across generations that live in other countries. Switzerland has an ethnic identity, even if it is multiple, and a high level of solidarity because it is grounded in the union of clear-cut and numerous differences.

The secular success of the Swiss model has lent encouragement to the European. However, the European has not simply made it up; Europe, and with it the European model, already existed. Europe brings myths and archetypes with it, some of them dating Europe as an Asian peninsula. (Compare Hesiod's *Catalogue of Women*, 19; Herodotus's *Histories* IV,45; and Ovid's *Metamorphoses* II, 833ff. and III, 1ff.) The myth is that of the Princess Europa, which as myth projected itself out from Asia into new territory. The archetype is that of the union of opposites, specifically an archetype of unity within diversity.

The ethnic identity which results is something that escapes all preceding definitions, based on blood or language, religion or territory. But probably it is more genuine, because it returns to the origins of the ethnic idea. *Ethnos* is a Greek word. The Greeks—divided into a host of tiny principalities predisposed to hate and fight each other, yet knowing full well that they comprised one people—were the first to realize they possessed this unifying quality. It was no accident that they created more myths than any other ancient people; myths are in fact the expression through images of this communal element.

What is ethnic identity, if not a society of earth, blood, language or religion? It is precisely what the Greeks taught by remaining Greek even when living in Persia or speaking Phoenician or converting to Christianity: it is the possession of a communal project, which gives meaning to speaking that language, living in that territory, and so on (45). A project, we would add, which expresses itself through images in the unified body of a highly differentiated mythology.

The Greeks were the first to synthesize opposites, to establish at one and the same time unity and multiformity.

Speaking about the Greeks is the same as speaking about antiquity. Nevertheless, even from the viewpoint of modern international politics there is no contradiction in this regard in simultaneously reinforcing union and fragmentation. In fact, there is perfect harmony between this perspective and the recent development of life globally. At the time the United Nations was born, the Earth's nations numbered 76. Today there are 192. As countries have multiplied, so have companies. It used to be that such developments could not have occurred simultaneously. Small countries were not born because, in the Darwinian manner, they were gobbled up by larger ones. Because with protectionism their internal economies remained too small to admit of any significant growth and prosperity. With globalization, things have changed. Global economy means that everyone does business with everyone else; even for the tiniest country its market is the world. Everyone specializes, and whoever does it better prospers more. Everyone takes part in a universal union, while developing their particular quality; countries divide along political lines precisely while conjoining their economic lives. In reality we forget that economics is driven by psychology, or better, by the human psyche. Additionally, the psyche resists a splitting of opposites, finding it unnatural for anything to express only its singularity. The psyche seeks its own completion.

Europe is the coffer which has opened to endow the world with this exemplary treasure: the tendency toward unity and differentiation at the same time. A victorious example, but one that is thoroughly debatable. Debatable not only from an economic viewpoint, but because aggregate commerce has a hand in both poverty and enrichment. It is debatable also because—from the viewpoint of myths and psychic images, which must accompany such great changes given that the psyche perceives them as neither alien nor monstrous—this collective transformation is running too fast in the opposite direction, toward the opposition between particular and universal. That is, this collective transformation is stretching its symbols to breaking point, threatening to sunder them into worn and chipped fragments that cannot be cemented once again into mythic wholeness.

Perhaps it was simply too ambitious, within the brief intervals for constituting the European Union, to compound myth and idea, and archetype and symbol, in a single figure, as a container of the opposites. Who imagines himself capable of lending a hand to the human psyche? Truly capable, that is, of holding together in the human mind both unity and multiplicity, or that which is reserved to God, who alone can be one and three at the same time?

These questions are too much for us, and we shall leave them unanswered. They belong to religion rather than to the psychology of myth and with it to the vast but contingent problem of founding Europe. We shall, however, begin to understand why the coming-together of Europe is neither accompanied by an escort of rekindled myths—myths that nevertheless persisted through the oldest European literature—nor by feelings of belonging to a shared territory—which all the same were described already by Herodotus.

It is this question to which we might be ready to give a preliminary, simplistic answer. Books on mythology all but ignore the myth of Europa, and historical studies draw up a nearly wholesale indictment of European history because, after a century of massacres brought on by European wars carried out in the name of belonging to one's country, it is taken for granted that only good business dealings will create the country to which we shall belong—in fact will *be* the shared country we shall belong to.

It therefore goes unspoken that Europe will be the European economy. There is truth in this rationale, which, however, neatly snaps shut the portfolio without looking into the psychology that opens and closes it. Because, if the basis for economics is made up of psychic activity, the collective psyche, in turn, is the nurse of mythology. At its birth, before any political, military or economic power comes into play, a country is unified by the power of myth.

So, what has the myth of Europa spoken? May we find allusions to the fate of the European earth in the destiny of the Princess Europa?

A sequence of abductions prepares the way for the fate of Europe: a chain of destinies enforced by violence, and vendettas exchanged between the shores of Europe and the Mediterranean Near East. Robert Calasso's *The Marriage of Cadmus and Harmony* (46) opens precisely with a reconstruction of this chain. Furthermore it occurs to us that the unexpected success of this story, apparently recondite, signifies the readiness of the European unconscious to listen once more to this ancient history.

According to Herodotus (I.1-2), some Phoenicians who were trading in Greece kidnapped Io, daughter of King Inacus; and the Greeks, by way of reprisal, kidnapped Europa, daughter of the Phoenician King Agenor (the names differ depending on the version). But the Herodotean version is already a historical-political interpretation. Of greatest interest to us is first of all the mythical version as such. The myth puts it this way:

> Europa was strolling on the seashore with a few other girls. From on high Zeus saw her and took a fancy to her. He assumed the likeness of a majestic white bull and manifested himself in her presence. Seduced by the power which offered itself so mildly, Europa draped flowers over the powerful beast and dared to mount his back from behind. The bull, at first so docile, lunged into a run down the beach, flung himself into the waves and made for the open sea.
>
> In the most popular reproductions, Europa is shown grasping a horn with one hand to keep herself upright while with the other she holds her garment rippling in the sea breeze. The god consummated his love once he had reached Crete, where Europa then married King Asterius, who, being without an heir, adopted Minos, Radamanthus and Sarpedon as his sons.

Desperate over the disappearance of his daughter, Agenor sends out his son Cadmus in search of his sister. According to the myth, from Cadmus came Thebes and the Theban Cycle, and thence the bloody vine of Greek tragedy. According to Herodotus (V.58), the Greeks, who still lacked an alphabet, adopted the Phoenician one from Cadmus' pilgrimage. Readapting it, they created the Greek alphabet, from which come all the alphabets of Europe. Already at first glance the rape of Europa is loaded with consequences and symbols.

Therefore, somewhat delicately, let me venture to do something with the various colours and forms here—the girl gathering flowers—without turning it, by all other accounts, into a leap one day into the saddle for a ride to the Occident. Where these colours and forms are given a solid throne and a royal function. Where girl-Europa becomes European earth. I shall make the irresistible push towards artificial and technical construction, those means which often get out of one's hands and forget the ends they are meant to serve, as so many European legends tell us. That tendency was already represented in antiquity by Minos, who had brought Daedalus to his court, the prototype of inventors.

This something—idea, inspiration, archetype—had its origin in Asia but came to be realised fully only on the new ground to which it gave its name. Even its power originated in Asia. As was the case with the idea of empire itself, which the Greeks loathed since they mistrusted absolute power and force, preferring encounters between men of equal dignity and the competition or battles between small city-states. Yet one day Alexander, who nonetheless remained, and wished to remain, Greek, decided to cobble together the greatest empire in the world and to receive the divine honours due to the emperors of Persia. As a result the opposites came together for the first time, the differentiation of the Greek mind and the unity of oriental power.

From the time of the Persian empire, in fact, the myth sought to give birth to itself, to transform itself from an unconscious image into a collective reality. In the myth Europa could not exist without the bull, nor the bull without Europa. The animal's power had no meaning without the delicacy of those flowers, just as unification by force would be meaningless without differentiation. But differentiation would simply degenerate into fragmentation and dispersal without the force that could hold it together.

Like Europa on the bull, through millennia the idea of empire has continued its march from East to West. While on such a journey it has brought tragedy (like the Theban Cycle) together with conceptual development (such as the birth of the alphabet) and technical development (like those precociously sponsored by Minos). In this march the idea has sought to embrace various sets of opposites: Asian origins with European destinations, unity with diversity. In antiquity, Persia moved upon the West; between the middle ages and the modern era it built the Turkish Ottoman Empire; finally, in our own day Russia dressed up as the Soviet Union of Socialist Republics. All three of these powers narrowly missed achieving their objectives, and all of them failed because they did not know how to make themselves truly unified and universal with respect to plurality and diversity. The opposites remained split and unity stifled differentiation.

It is remarkable to think that these precedents—brought together in the brief but traumatic experience of the fascisms that would have united Europe with a force that obliterates all differences—would have to weigh so heavily on the so-called collective unconscious. And that probably by now, in opposing itself to such violence, the principle of differentiation must overtake that of unification. We are now sensing a renaissance of the smaller countries and local customs. The opposites between countries are once again difficult to reconcile because one of them has been privileged while the other has been repressed. Therefore the typical citizen finds himself in harmony with the search for greater prosperity and political stability through Europe, but while agreeing to give as little as possible to any unifying thrust: agreeing to give up on European myths, symbols and rituals without wholly doing away with them. Agreeing to midwife the birth of Europe, the first event of its kind, without an accompanying panoply of imagery and deep feeling. All because the pace of change—of many changes—has by now become so dreadful that the ordinary citizen would rather take refuge in some reassuring corner of local reality.

Permit me here a little dip into current events. In a setting beyond the ordinary, because there one can see where the remnants of myths, rituals and the clashes between peoples have taken to hiding out: in the soccer championships. The finals of the 1998 World Cup had France playing against Brazil and was seen on television by an immense number of Italians because Italy's team had just been eliminated. Since identification runs rife among sports fans, you may believe if I ask whether some part of their interest did not rise from the match between a European team and one from a far-off continent. I eagerly awaited the game's aftermath, since the fan is more interesting than the game. Yet at match's end, nothing then happened. Only the usual traffic noise from below. Following such an important and symbolic event—the triumph of the French over the unequalled Brazilians was uproarious and unexpected—there was not even one hundredth the noise from auto horns that *always* celebrates a victory, not only by the national team but any Italian team whatsoever. Since a few thousand French and French-speaking people live in Milan, the miniscule blatting of horns was undoubtedly *theirs*, not *ours*.

I called friends on the telephone to double-check. Not only in Rome and Florence, but also in London and Brussels, Zurich and Vienna, nothing whatsoever happened.

In Milan one failed to see not only the French *tricolore* but also the EU flag, whether on cars or balconies, either on the evening of the victory or the following day.

Not one of the newspapers or television stations which remind us daily that we belong to Europe and which, in fact, are the most pro-European among European countries, not one of the institutions which by law now showcase the EU banner, yes, not one single mass medium and no single public figure, after years of spouting *the name* of Europe, had thought of celebrating *in the name* of Europe.

Not one of them remembered—as they would have with any national tournament—that in a championship which included every continent, the smallest of them won three out of four places. Football is ritual and myth, but Europe silently drowns them. Europe is nothing but the European economy. Europe is the same old Germans and of course the amazing Irish, who are paying our debts. Europe is other people.

A talk presented at the conference on *The Symbolic Imaginary* in Marsala, 1998.

(45) J. Cuisenier, *Ethnologie de l'Europe*. PUF, Paris, 1991.
(46) Roberto Calasso, *The Marriage of Cadmus and Harmony* (1988). Knopf, New York 1993.

Part Four
Tragic Thought

Chapter Fourteen

The *Agamemnon* and the Contemporary Presence of Tragedy

On those obligatory school trips to visit the remains of classical Greece, little or no instruction is devoted to the Greek moral code. As if Greece, which has every reason to be called the foundation of the entire West, may be wholly accounted for through its myths, religions and sublime art, with no attention to its ethics.

As happened in ancient civilization, the Greeks were quite far from possessing a definite moral code; and as for their religion, not to mention their idea of immortality, it seems like a country of the absurd. Nevertheless, for the want of a real *code* they supplied a highly powerful, fully present ethical *inspiration*. If they lacked rational rules, a profound feeling always attended their actions and lent them unity. Such inspiration can obligate one more completely than any code, because its ordering principle lies beyond words and can only be weakened by rational discussion. It is emotion, felt almost physically, without becoming an abstract idea.

To possess glory beyond measure is a grave matter. Zeus keeps watch on high, hurling his lightning at everything that overreaches its condition (Aeschylus, *Agamemnon* 468ff); this theme is also dear to Herodotus, for example in the *Histories* VII.10). Agamemnon, who returns in triumph from Troy, hangs back, finally debarks, and sets foot in his palace, treading the ceremonial red carpet which Queen Clytemnestra has rolled out for him. His words communicate anxiety, leading us to imagine tremors in the hands and sweat on the royal brow (914ff.). Here, more than with the assassination of the king, the drama's true violence comes into play. When Agamemnon suddenly falls for the Queen's flattery and willingly goes through with the reception whose garish celebrations are typically bestowed on barbarian kings, we realize that Clytemnestra has checkmated him and won. He toppled his own existence as a moral being long before falling under the axe.

Agamemnon's syndrome is the terror of *hýbris*, and into *hýbris* are gathered all the evils of the Hellenic mind. By that term the Greeks meant an excess of pride and satisfaction: the exercise of unrestrained will. Without *hýbris* Aeschylus is simply inconceivable, and with it, perhaps, tragedy itself and the whole mentality of the Greeks. Yet without the shaping mind of the Greek attitude we would be cut off from our roots and in a certain way would become incomprehensible to ourselves. Probably for that reason *hýbris* is actually quite real to us and can speak more to us than even our own modern sins.

The counterpart of *hýbris* is *phthónos*: the hatred which the gods have for human beings who achieve a great deal or want too much, and also the natural consequence of *hýbris*: *némesis*, that impersonal mechanism of justice which lays low those who climb too high.

To Prometheus, who inaugurates the whole cycle of improvement in the human condition, the chorus suggests only one moral: justice bows to *némesis* (*Prometheus* 936). *Némesis* is the distributive justice moved by the anger of the gods, by which any person overreaching is inevitably cut down to size. A justice that is ancestor to that Christian principle contained in the Sermon on the Mount: whoever exalts himself shall be brought low.

Finally, in more contemporary, simple and clear terms, *hýbris* is the limit of human will. With Prometheus begins a craving and quest for unlimited gratification which Western people have carried with them all over the globe. Aeschylus knew this craving and feared it. Therefore he will celebrate in *the Persians* the victory of the barbarians, describing their sorrows but holding his tongue about Greek glory. (For essentially the same reason, he stipulated that his tombstone identify him not as a writer but only as a hoplite who had fought at Marathon.)

Until Aeschylus, descriptions of the human lot were entrusted to the feeling for limits. In the poems of Mimnermus (Diehl 2), in Glaucus' description of his own origins in the *Iliad* (VI.146) and according to the wisdom of the old men in the *Agamemnon* (line 79), human beings are like leaves: fragile, destined to live briefly, particles that vanish into the whole. It is difficult to imagine a self-representation more unlike the one we give of ourselves, we modern Europeans. In equal degrees, our monotheistic roots, which would make us into the image and likeness of God, and our cult of progress, tied to Enlightenment optimism, have made us familiar with the temptation to live without any sense of limits.

The Greek gods face in the other direction. For the Greeks they watched over the observances due to them by limited human beings: in point of being not simply strangers to human love, but openly merciless. Their wrath towards each outstanding human possession or happiness prohibited progress, and in fact authorized regression; in Hesiod's *Works and Days* the Golden Age of the human condition falls off, declining to the Age of Iron.

Christian optimism was destined to overturn this divine function. Rather than wrath it practices affiliation. In this new relationship it also overturns the human attitude. Instead of going in fear of God's wrath Christians did precisely what for the Greeks was forbidden: they imitated God (*imitatio Christi*). The saints seem almost to live in symbiosis with God. The expectations of modern secular progressivism essentially continue down the same road. The morality of *hýbris* has disappeared, and the unwavering respect for limits has transformed itself into a legitimization of the unlimited.

In essence the West has had two sacred texts: the book of tragedy and the Bible. The first would have humankind bow down, while the second would have it rise. Humanity, however, began to stand up not only when it converted to Christianity, but earlier, when it left off taking part in the ritual of tragedy.

On all these grounds I have tried to engage with the following question: when and along what avenues have we in the West lost the sense of limitation and acquired that cult of betterment or progress which was *hýbris* itself for the Greeks, the founders and prototypes of our civilization? For our purposes it will suffice to recall that the major turnaround—from the cult of limits to a cult of the unbounded—occurred precisely in the age of Pericles, the century of the Hellenes' greatest achievements, during which tragedy fell silent and left the stage. It is as if all the great thinkers flocked around *hýbris* to study it and condemn it, because they were infinitely more drawn than other persons to the examining of things. At the same time, it is as if they would exalt tragedy (part of the Dionysian cult, we must remember, and not simply a performance) by creating a grandiose collective ritual for the containment of this temptation and for the restoration of strict limits.

Therefore it was for quite another and conclusive reason after the fifth century, when the momentum of progressivism became irresistible, that tragedy disappeared. Tragedy framed a vision of the world that was marked by a respect for limits. It is useless to celebrate the rituals of limitation when limits in fact are vanishing, just as it would become meaningless to insist dogmatically on the Ptolemaic system— one more religious vision of the world based upon limits— when it had been set aside by ships which had sailed around the world.

Our argument asks us firmly to grasp the point that tragedy, above all in Aeschylus, constituted a solemn affirmation and contemplation of limits. Yet this was the case precisely because the tragedians deeply understood, curbed and condemned *hýbris*. Tragedy therefore made room for and gave all due respect to human ambivalence, which under any title whatsoever can be called dramatic.

In my view the great interest in the relations which moderns have with tragedy rises first of all from a repression. We turn away from the nostalgia for limits and ambivalence observed by tragedy, which progress has set aside in the first instance to further unlimited progress, and in the second to foster a monovalent rationalism, as necessary for the Judeo-Christian commandments (let your word be *Yes, yes*, or *No, no*) as it is for the scientific method, which provides for precise and necessary formulations.

The great and by no means accidentally ambivalent interest which the modern era pays to such a tiring, costly, unproductive, minimally scientific and in fact pre-Enlightenment procedure as analysis, springs from something very simple and indeed quite similar. We need to feel free of the obligation immediately and always to come up with solutions; we need the possibility of remaining dramatically ambivalent; we also need to recognize that our lives are given the marks of destiny and are given over to mystery, though not stripped of dignity; and to accept the limits that enlarge our sense of failure and of 'having to' overcome them, which the modern cult of productivity would foist upon us. If we succeed in framing this kinship between the mentality of analysis and the mentality of Greek tragedy, we shall also have suggested a profound motive for the fascination, ever since its birth, which analysis has turned toward tragedy more thoroughly than to any other form of expression (47). We shall take this up at greater length in a moment. Let us restrict ourselves here to recalling that our civilization has produced two opposing descriptions of the world, two narrative structures: the tragic and the post-tragic, whether in written narratives, film, or the comics.

To these descriptions there correspond two relationships with the world. The first, observant of limits, therefore is only descriptive, in fact contemplative. The second is acquisitive, accumulative, and fact-hungry. Nothing whatsoever escapes this contrast between our antiquity and our modernity. Naturally certain great visionary enterprises, such as Dante's and Goethe's, transcend any simple contrast between the two world-descriptions, in a high synthesis. But it is significant that these are utterly singular events that do not go toward making up a genre.

Likewise the fact that in tragedy the plot is already given, whist the narrative art of later ages has the task of inventing it, is no accidental matter due exclusively to technical literary developments. It stands already prefigured in the origin of their opposed structures. Tragedy furnishes only narration, contemplation, emotion, while the event being described is always just-so. By its very nature tragedy implies limit, the acceptance of *anánke*, of that which already exists or had been prescribed. The hero constantly faces death, the paradigm of all limitations, nor does he try to get around it. Hemmed in by such crushing limitations, his action does not, however, appear futile. In the narrow passage that is left to him, the hero wagers his freedom in a style that remains public while consisting of private feelings; the same holds for Achilles as for Hector, for Eteocles as for Orestes.

Post-tragic narration instead furnishes, time and again, splices and jointures, the story and the event of storytelling. The modest revivals of classical themes neither succeeded in attaining the same heights nor easily refrained from the temptation to ring changes on them. Each new possible storyline meant boundless freedom, first for the characters acting in them, and then for the author and the meanings which the new story had inspired. It is also significant in this regard that Euripides, introducing variations on mythical themes, as well as new plot solutions and gods who intervened in the action, stretched the boundaries of tragedy to their maximum and marked the advent of a new genre.

Let us now verify whether the two differing versions of the world; the one inspired by limits and the other by *hýbris*, speak discordant languages.

A primary distinction within any language separates transitive from intransitive action. The first passes—makes a transit—to an object; the second remains in the neighbourhood of the subject. This quality can be used to indicate precisely the difference which concerns us here. Tragedy is intransitive, in fact it is reflexive. Its action does not change the basis of things, but remains near its subject or returns to it. Without question, tragedy and the epic from which it originates know *hýbris* very well indeed. This pattern, however, describes a circle, within which it visibly holds action to a limit, and then returns to its origin. The *hýbris* of Agamemnon incites that of Achilles, his pride in Patroclus, over whose spoils Hector's arrogance will catch fire; thereafter the *hýbris* will return upon Achilles. Agamemnon will meet up with it again in the *Oresteia*, the Aeschylean cycle of tragedies which opens with the murder of Agamemnon as the work of his wife Clytemnestra and her lover, followed by Orestes' vendetta, who kills his mother so as to render justice to his father. Even after Clytemnestra's death has been accomplished following her husband's, it will be found that none of these urgent human actors has obtained anything. Only destiny has fulfilled its ends.

On another occasion (48) we shall ask if the same kind of development for Oedipus, customarily treated as the paradigm of enclosure or incest, is not the paradigm of a destiny that encloses *hýbris* within the higher limit of mystery. Tiresias in fact admonishes Oedipus for wishing at all costs to penetrate to the nature of his own beginnings. Preoccupied with a rationalistic *hýbris*, the king will not listen to him and transgresses every limit in his need to shed light on things; but when he learns the truth, he single-handedly condemns himself to darkness by blinding himself.

Hýbris, which stamps the vision of the world following the death of tragedy and its ritual observance, no longer knew these fated limits. Without question it is transitive; it always demands an object, it is acquisitive and wants the accusative case. Once permanently installed as a reporter on new objects out there, *hýbris* attacks everything and, if it does not manage to master it, rejects it and converts it into an antagonist. The post-tragic description of the world is unable to contemplate suffering as such, because it sunders good from evil; Brecht, in contrast to how Aeschylus handled the Persians, never could have written a play about the sorrows of the Nazis.

To be sure, it would be going too far to say that after tragedy our civilization remained unconscious of *hýbris*. The principle moral systems inevitably occupied themselves with it. The point is that, for the most part, there may very well be *antagonists* without there necessarily being any *limitations*. Yes, Christianity and Marxism pursue opposed tendencies toward human omnipotence. They do this not so much in themselves, however, but only distinguishing according to the object at which their omnipotence aims. Wanting more is not always bad; it is good if it wants good things. What mounts an effective battle against *hýbris*, therefore, is no longer any absolute limit but rather what love, solidarity, and political renewal can manage to work out from time to time. No interdict, in fact, ever has any effect on the implicit omnipotence, or *hýbris*, of a boundless devotion to holiness or to a political cause. These visions of the world are therefore transitive in the way that *hýbris* is, building themselves up just as their adversaries do. They conceal a sly victory on the part of *hýbris* within the cosmic and triumphal character of their eschatologies.

Anticipating things somewhat, it is possible to think that analysis today attracts so much ambivalent attention and so much energy because it is the only cultural instrument and also the only vision of the world—since it is about so much more than a cluttered and ineffective therapeutic technique— that turns unproductively to the creation of limits; in fact is opposed singly and heroically to productivity. If it is true, as it is, that ambivalence is in itself mysterious; if it is also true, as it is, that mystery and meaning are closely related, then we may imagine that analysis may be so widespread not because of a spontaneous upsurge in psychic suffering but because it deals with the mystery of suffering not necessarily as an illness in need of cure or an enemy to do away with.

Freud has been hastily popularized as the champion of an Ego that will supplant the Id. In this light he has been able to play the role of impresario to a *hýbris* of rationality. Yet to do him justice one needs to remember that in Freud, too, it is necessary to distinguish between mind and temperament. Freud's temperament is in fact tragic. For the tragic temperament human will is a small affair; its ransom comes not from making a small thing a little larger, but in recognizing in it a great dignity. Faithful to this temperament, Freud dedicated himself to relativizing the ego's imperialism, on which Western civilization is founded. The Copernican and Darwinian revolutions have been the two chief deflations administered to this omnipotent anthropocentrism derived from the biblical relationship with God. Earth and the human species are miniscule stages in the evolutionary continuum. In much the same way the conscious ego is a still fragile stage in the development of the psyche. Every day, but above all every night, it retires from the field to go back into the unconscious.

The ego-centered person stocked up with conscious willpower is essentially the puppet on the strings of movements begun infinitely earlier, cosmic as much as zoological and psychological. Jung will complete this relativization of rational man by immeasurably extending the reach of the so-called unconscious, which pre-exists all conscious experience and, long before obtaining personal memory, already contains traces of a collective one.

If we have had to reconstruct in summary fashion what the field of action is for analysis and its cognitive revolution, it has been to banish all equivocation. In the last few years, debates in several countries over the legal recognition of psychotherapeutic activity, and over-productivity, the reimbursement of costs and so on, the major media have consistently described analysis from the viewpoint of efficacy, giving one the impression that analysis is a matter of a rather complicated but supremely logical instrument which heals precisely by restoring rationality to a bewildered ego.

In reality it is precisely the opposite. If analysis in general supports a certain recovery of will and complex coherence in the person, this comes about as it were by accident. In fact it results, paradoxically but understandably, from the long, wearisome labour of attending to and revealing the unconscious and pre-logical components that make up by far the greater part of the psyche. If I have occasionally and provocatively called analysis a 'pre-Enlightenment' affair, I certainly did not intend to make it the handiwork of people who are ignorant of modern culture. I meant that they have inflicted one more blow upon our likeness to the biblical God, compelling us to observe how even in the adult human being the stratum of consciousness—and the will that derives from it—is a subtle and intermittent superstructure, that floats on a sea of emotions and heedless images. Analysis therefore does not lend a hand to rational consciousness by reinforcing it. On the contrary, it brings back to the psyche a relatively natural equilibrium by restoring legitimacy to its more infantile and primitive aspects. When we take up the fight against irrational impulses or terrifying nightmares and obsessions, we know that the appeal to conscious intentions is not only futile but counterproductive. Only by respecting and penetrating to the meaning of these phantasms, only by accepting that the fact that ambivalence is stronger than the will, can we come once more to being at a certain kind of peace with ourselves.

Is this not the clearest and most explicit refutation of modern *hýbris*? Of that arrogance of will, desire and rationality authorized by today's myth of eternal progress? Is analysis not the very thing that acknowledges the absurd as being built into our nature, and the will as a fragile and impotent superimposition, and mystery as a truth frequently superior to rational truth? Is it that this truth knows how mortal dangers lie not outside man but in his unexamined passions and his *hýbris*; that restores peace not by intervening decisively in life but by managing to contemplate it, to be forgiving towards it, and to hear the story it is telling? This disarmed therapy, what is it if not the transposition into modern terms of the ancient tragic description of the universe?

To be sure, tragedy is on intimate terms with more than analysis. It was a public occasion linked to a polytheistic cult and the rituals that honoured Dionysus. Tragedy, however, in contrast to how we imagine it today by analogy with the commonly shared genres of narrative, *is not* a text composed by an author who hopes for the success and enduring fame of his work. Tragedy is not some libretto to be sung *ad infinitum*. Originally it was meant to take place once only, in a single performance. Therefore tragedy is a profound emotion, to be shared with as many people as can be present. An unrepeatable emotion, contained within the limits of a single enactment: exactly like the analytic event today.

As has been said, the old gods are not dead but have come back, as illnesses. The transcendent experience today is possible only in privacy; and the one faith still universally shared is in science and technology, to which the modern mind expects psychotherapy to belong. Here then is where the ancient rite of tragedy—which exorcized *hýbris* among the people who knew it, the Greeks—comes in again disguised as a particular therapeutic modality for people who more than anything must face *hýbris* and fight it. Therefore it may be true that, while on one hand modernity encourages *hýbris*, yet on the other it restores limits for human beings through new forms of consciousness that make relative its centrality and will: first the Copernican revolution, then the Darwinian, and now the analytic.

Analysis does not suggest specific interventions because it recognizes the ephemeral quality of the will. It proposes only to arrive at the end of analysis. The end of analysis is the goal of analysis, and vice versa (49). At the terminus this goal or end will come back to the subject, like the outcome of tragedy; it will be restored therein because (as with tragedy) it is rigorously intransitive. In the meantime it will have described and contemplated the meaning of events, disclosed feeling more than rationality, and made things accessible rather than changing them. There are no objects outside of us worth the trouble of conquest; there is only an inner task to which to remain faithful: this is the translation of that cumbersome technical principle according to which, in analysis, one needs to practice *acting in* (resting with the inwardness of the event, accepting it as intransitive) and refraining from *acting out*.

All of which for the modern Westerner has certain precedents in the Greek world. Yet while the rational tradition of Western medicine signs on with the continuity and categories of Socratic philosophy, analysis attempts to enter the space of mystery, of terror, but also of that contemplative solace which raised tragedy to its greatness and of which every succeeding age has preserved the piercing memory.

A paper read at the conference on *The Concept of Limits* in Catania, 1994.

(47) Chapter 17 of this book.
(48) Chapter 15 of this book.
(49) 'The *fine* [feminine] of analysis is the *fine* [masculine] of analysis.' (Translator's note.)

Chapter Fifteen

A Different Oedipus

Oedipus the King can be seen, among other things, as the dramatic emblem of an encounter between two mental outlooks, one of which nurtured Greek antiquity while the other undid it, and both of which Greek civilization has left successive civilizations to shoulder as best they can. On one side is the old culture, in which truth is myth, mystery, deep and irrational emotion, a respect for the undefined and a terror of the infinite. On the other side is the knowledge and consciousness that wish to go on perfecting themselves without end, and truth as a consensual rationality that wants to go on growing at the expense of the emotions: in a word, *hýbris*, which even at the time of Sophocles was exploding on the cognitive plane, with the exodus from myth to philosophy, and with that turbulent political transition of the *póleis* from self-sufficiency to imperial conquest. These two poles, between which truth is held in dispute, were represented by Oedipus, a king, and Tiresias, a prophet.

Concerning Oedipus we shall argue roughly as follows: this tragic hero has no sexual problem. Oedipus was not attracted to his mother. Not simply because he did not know that Jocasta was his mother, but because he marries her only in order to become king. Instead, Oedipus has a problem of consciousness. He wants to illuminate, to clarify, and to rationally reconstruct events with the perspicacity of the modern police commissioner charged with solving a major criminal case. Instead of the enigma, however, he encounters a mystery; the first submits to reason, whereas the second brings together—into an invincible tragic background— ancient drama and modern anxiety. The analyst dedicates himself to delving into tragedy more than any other kind of literature, precisely because he feels himself at one with something of this mysterious invincibility.

I shall briefly summarize the main points of the play, by looking for that thread along which the Oedipus-Tiresias encounter comes into view. Sophocles certainly realized that history was placing itself on the side of rationality and *hýbris*. He responded to this new arrogance of the mind by showing that truth is not the same as knowledge. Living in truth is in fact a way of living in mystery—accepting mystery not only as having certain occulted workings but also as possessing a specific and irreplaceable value: 'How terrible knowledge is', says Tiresias to Oedipus, 'when that knowledge is useless to the one who has it' (315-16).

Whoever is familiar with such distinctions will immediately set this idea of mystery alongside Jung's idea of the symbol, understood as an original and creative product of the unconscious, in contrast to the occulted or encoded notion of Freud, which Jung thought it better to call a sign. Just as the symbol which has not been interpreted can retain a higher meaning than one which has been explained and reduced to excessive flatness by decoding, so the vital meaning of mystery can best dwell in its own obscurity and ambiguity, which the mind's abilities can only partly inquire into and uncover.

The encounter between these two poles in *Oedipus Rex* is not only a conflict between two mentalities which stand for two epochs one of which follows the other. It is also the emblem of a perennial internal dynamic, whereby the desire for rational knowledge overflows into the *hýbris* of knowing (according to Jung the prototype for every sin of modern man), even going so far as to punish itself. Every attitude that pursues knowledge too unilaterally ends sooner or later by unconsciously activating its own opposite (the movement of enantiodromia); and these psychological components together contribute to historical circumstances, in an intricate tangle which is difficult to unravel.

Rationality as an exclusive faith is only apparently the supremacy of the intellect: more fundamentally it is a visceral passion for revealing what, fed only by its own kind of rational 'truth', can turn into blindness.

At the outset of the drama, Oedipus solemnly promises to hunt down the murderer of Laius and also, with the same promise, declares with subjective finality and psychological ignorance that 'not for the sake of far-off relatives do I want to get rid of this pollution, but for my own sake. Whoever murdered him might choose with the same hand to kill me too' (139-40).

We, who on hearing these words already know that the murderer and the king are the same person, perceive in this identity of the subject with his object an inner problem: according to the principle of enantiodromia, whoever unilaterally takes the side of the *persona* (the socially ennobling role) will fall victim to the *shadow* (socially inadmissible impulses). Oedipus feels radically invested in his role as king and judge, and he sides with the god Apollo and the dead king, condemning the culprit (244-45); he lauds the deceased as 'the best of kings' (257), and we listeners, knowing that Laius was anything but stainless, already tremble at this unnatural glorification, which fulfills itself unconsciously in the terrible truth of accomplished fact when Oedipus proclaims that he will fight for Laius as if he were his own father (264).

The conflict that follows between Oedipus and Tiresias is an irreconcilable encounter between knowledge and wisdom. The king mocks the prophet's blindness (388), while Tiresias observes that Oedipus, though he possesses eyes, cannot see evil and therefore will lose them (414). The king boasts about the lucidity of his mind (*gnóme*) with which he bested the Sphinx (398), while the prophet concedes that nature in its complexity may, in its wisdom, appear to be stupid (*morós*, 436) in the eyes of a rationalist.

The listener cannot but notice in Oedipus an irascible one-sidedness, typical of *hýbris*, and consequently returns to the riddle of the Sphinx: had Oedipus gotten to the bottom of an enigma or simply worked out a puzzle? Had he decoded a sign or murdered a symbol? This listener recalls that the destructive presence of the Sphinx constituted submission to a castrating and terrible feminine principle, one that had been mandated by the goddess Hera. Oedipus certainly had not overcome the profound menace that hung over Thebes, so much so that now, during his reign, the city lay once again under a divinely ordained plague. Oedipus, then, leaving the underlying mystery intact, has simply solved a problem with his rational faculties in the way that someone on a trip blandly takes a crack at the *Weekly Puzzler*.

Oedipus is concerned with *solutions*, which are meaningful only if they prove something. Tiresias is concerned with *truth*, which does not necessarily speak in that way. Thence rises an irremediable conflict, because the two forms of knowing, which do not move on the same plane, will never meet. Then comes the straying of Oedipus, when he will begin to realize that one aspect of knowing, moving on a higher plane—or a deeper one—escapes him. Is it true that the prophet knows about the time of Laius' murder, since he still has not spoken up? Tiresias eludes the usual categories of time, as well as those of positive law, according to which the reticent testimony of a killer makes him an accomplice. To our eyes, the mental one-sidedness of Oedipus begins to coincide with the singular one-sidedness of his body: Oedipus, whose feet were pinned together at the ankles from the first days of his life (giving him the meaning of his name: 'swollen foot'), has transferred his vitality by way of compensation into his head.

Yet, as we know from analytic experience, rationality that takes up defenses behind a one-sided line of communication, in short order declines into rationalization, not at all serving to solve the fundamental error, but precisely to reinforce and conceal it.

Jocasta, the mother and wife—the principal feminine figure who pinned the feet of her newborn and now symbolically immobilizes him one more time, who strangles a true growth and autonomy, because she brings back into her body what left it as a child—rationalizes the limited consciousness out of which she prepares the reconstruction of Oedipus' past and the murder of Laius. She wishes to retain a strict knowledge of externals, refusing all awareness of the psychic depths that she feels, whether they flare up in her or in Oedipus.

A prophecy, she reveals, had told Laius that he would be killed by his own son, but Laius was murdered by bandits; and as for the son, no sooner was he born than his ankles were pinned and he was abandoned on a mountainside. Precisely these revelations, which come close to the final truth, come to be used in confirming what seems to be the truth. In that *seeming truth* we meet up with a forerunner simultaneously of either the structure of a modern crime novel or of the defense mechanisms mobilized by rationalization in the face of profound emotions.

But when Jocasta evokes the crossroads (716) where Laius was murdered, the mind of Oedipus is thunderstruck by images. Where from? Perhaps from the two meanings always present in a truth? From the good and the bad that are always possible in an action? From the ambivalence, from the conscious side and the unconscious, that is always contained in the psyche? From the encounter cobbled together between the two chunks of the symbol? The symbol in fact is not only a modern thing, but also that ancient object intentionally broken into two pieces in order to entrust it to persons who live far apart, which lets them fit the two matching pieces together again. Just as with the symbol in modern psychology, the ancient object was greater than the sum of its parts.

Oedipus had been able to be a good and highly esteemed king only by artificially suppressing the crossroads in himself, letting only the mainstream way in him have any life, the stereotyped and incomplete images of the proper gentleman who comes to know his life without confronting either temptations or alternatives, and without meeting up with his 'other'.

In reality Oedipus had encountered the other exactly at that crossroads, not only the other as itself, the father as enemy, but the other in itself: the assassin. The displaced past returns not just to cross this threshold on whose closure the one-sidedness of the present was hinged. Oedipus remembers the doubt cast on his origins which, when he lived in Corinth, a drunken man had insinuated to him. Tormented, he went off to Delphi. However, the god of the bow and the lyre, Apollo, did not respond directly to the suppliant, for he speaks, as his paired attributes do, ambiguously. Asked about the past, he spoke of the future: Oedipus would marry his mother and slay his father.

And so Oedipus was propelled like a heedless fugitive toward his destination, as long as that energy carried him far from what he believed was his birthplace. Yet by now we know that one-sidedness sooner or later involves a paradoxical encounter with the contrary position. Just as a maniacal headlong high can finally be balanced out by the major upset of a depression, so the escape of Oedipus from his supposed birthplace will bring him exactly to his true origins, and his thrust toward an ever more rational vision will have him gradually round back on his point of departure, where darkness reigns instead of light, to the extent that finally the emotions no longer submit to control and blindness is no longer symbolic.

Even rational *hýbris*, however, even if until now reduced to a grotesque self-deception, is a chalice that will finally be drained to the last drop.

The same messenger who will introduce the final truth was used by Oedipus and Jocasta to hide it behind a curtain woven from partial and equivocal truth: the old king, Polybus, has died, and so Oedipus is no longer in danger of killing his own father. Labouring over this web, Oedipus does not escape pursuing another false trail, where rationalistic *hýbris* degenerates into a specific kind of interpretive *hýbris*, the kind thoroughly familiar to those acquainted with the sins of pride which turn up in analytic work. 'I have not killed Polybus', says Oedipus, 'at least if it is impossible to say that he died of longing [for me]' (969-70). Any road is a good road so long as it supports the isolated fragment of truth circumscribed by the intellect and runs away from the inclusive kind of question that every truth puts to its discoverer.

From that point on everything came to a head. Jocasta grasps the situation and, finally honest with herself (because the real sin between them has not been their sexual relationship as much as this form of insincerity), falls silent and tries to block Oedipus. He gives himself over evermore frantically to the guidance of *hýbris* and, throwing himself into knowing things at any price, even lets himself get there by way of another wrong trail: 'I shall know where I come from! Even if I come from slaves I will have no shame, for I know myself to be the son of a good fate' (*Tyche*; 1080-81).

Since he knew that he had raised himself to kingly rank, Oedipus seems to believe in a subjective fate, as if self-fashioned, stronger than the tragic and changeless destiny of the classical tradition. Faced with the same thing, Jocasta had spoken of fate as a paradigm of immutability (977), and listening to her one seems almost to hear an Enlightenment manifesto and to pull in some anticipation of free will. But through the workings of Sophocles' intentions, tied as they are to the depths of tragic meaning and inimical to the superficiality of the intellect, this claim exists to manifest its own opposite. The cognitive reasoning of Oedipus grows more violent, and resorts to violence even against the old manservant who knows how his king was born but avoids telling him the bad news which he knowingly contains.

The final revelation is incest: the inevitable punishment brought down on cognitive *hýbris* by the image of the necessary return to origins, of the symbolic impossibility of fertilizing with one's own *lógos* a truly new domain.

Oedipus assigned himself a pre-Enlightenment task, consisting already of accumulating knowledge in order to obtain progress. It resulted instead in a victory for mythical destiny, which sets singular human journeys back at zero by bringing everything back to the place from where it originated. In this circular journey Oedipus has lost along the way the great mythic and theological container: 'Now', he cries, 'I am without God' (*átheos*: 1360).

Destroyed by his own rational *hýbris*, Oedipus wishes to punish himself symbolically. He reacts to his own rationalistic excesses mythically, irrationally and destructively, completing the enantiodromia by blinding himself.

To all affected witnesses, ancient or modern, Oedipus continues to communicate a changeless principle: every life makes a wager at the crossroads where truth and reason meet, and whoever sets out on the journey knows that in their convergence these powers do not add themselves to each other but cancel each other out, unless and until they compound themselves into the higher unity of a symbol.

Presented at the national congress of the CIPA on *Mario Moreno and the Horizons of Analytical Psychology*. Published in *La Pratica Analitica* vol.10 no.11, 1995.

Chapter Sixteen

Unhappiness

So just who is unhappy? Let us try to reflect on this question.

The best fed and most opulent society in history has given birth to grave new shortages: scarcities that certainly existed beforehand but which now have assumed the dignity of problems, about which arguments are carried on in public. The paradox in fact is that we are talking not about a thing, as we would if we were talking about 'psychological illness' or 'depression', but about the absence of a thing; *un*-happiness.

There was a time when unhappiness could not be considered as an object of study, just as one did not study im-potence. Naturally, every epoch has conjured with desperate people or sexual problems, but only our own time has sanctioned a right to sexual potency and a right to happiness, which are the necessary presuppositions to their absence.

There is a great novelty in all this: the generalized awareness of human rights, initially sanctioned on the political level, is slowly penetrating into the psychic sphere in capillary fashion. The world of desires has been reshaped and rendered more complex by this diffusion of consciousness. The result is that today, in contrast to the past, we not only feel nostalgia for what has been, but we suffer nostalgia for what is possible: sadness over the lack of that which has never been and probably never will be.

The un-happiness/im-potence approach is intentionally extreme. In reality, in the case of a physical function we instinctively know what is lacking; not so with a psychic quality, above all with something as ineffable as happiness. And therewith the second obstacle: not only in dealing with our object must we deal with its opposite, but also our very object—happiness—is inexpressible.

If we had sought to individualize what the current notion is, the idea or personal experience of happiness, we would come up with nothing, due either to the total subjectivity of the definitions, or the large number of contexts in which these definitions operate. For some people, happiness is religious experience, for others it is philosophical; there are those who point to the presence of certain things, and those who value the absence of preoccupations or pain. Certainly our current literalism and consumerism tend always to bring up the happiness at satisfying one's needs, a relatively new idea.

In the absence of a universally valid definition, then, we must turn once more to the single reliable notion, the one that is retraceable through etymology. Our minds frequently maintain an unconscious familiarity with it, independently of the disappearance of original meanings from conscious memory.

A brief examination of etymology in the major European languages will confirm that even the languages in the main lines of descent—Germanic and Romance languages— mention happiness while starting from various points of view, but gradually come to a meaning that holds certain things in common.

The Italian *felice* derives from Latin *felicitas*, which in turn comes from the same root as *fecunditas*; in sum, happy and fertile are similar ideas to begin with.

The French *heureux* indicates happiness or good fortune in the moment at hand; the same for *bon-heur, heur* coming from the Latin *au)gurium* or presage, augury (whether good or bad).

The German *Glück(lich)* goes back to *Lücke* or exit, and indicates how a thing comes out, its good or bad ending (analogously to English *luck*, a good or bad fate).

Finally, English *happy(ness)* has come from *to happen*, to take place or come about (by chance), and therefore, from another side, still points to fate.

On closer examination, all these concepts have as their subtext a notion held in common: happiness depends upon the forces of nature, fate or the gods, in any case not on human ones. Happiness is a good fate, not something that one can do anything about. This was the constant conviction that pre-modern Europeans left understood or unspoken when examining the idea of happiness.

In turn, given the rigid separation between human and transcendent forces and the primacy of the latter in a pre-modern society, that unspoken conviction implied a warning: do not venture onto the field of happiness because no one is in charge of fate; do not take up with superior forces, jealous as they are of their prerogatives. Unlike moderns, people in antiquity or in primitive societies for the most part studiously avoided penetrating the territory of happiness. Some did this from generic, superstitious fear, out of respect for the metaphysical and non-human authority assigned to this sphere. Others did so from an explicit conviction that divine power prohibited it, that the divine therefore not only reserved the administration of happiness to itself, but also its enjoyment.

Behind these ideas lurks not so much the superstition of polytheism or of animism, as a psychological valuation that is profound and valid at all times: namely, that happiness, as the balance of these etymologies indicate, is not something that we can program any more than we can arrange fate or the weather, because it comes and goes at its own sweet will, like the rain or the wind. Rather it is an occasional quality with which we experiment, and fate the same. Therefore not only are we unable to organize it, we cannot even pursue it. The main motive for which instead, believe it though we may, and gaze at it as we do at the supermarket, rests probably in the confusion between happiness and the satisfaction of material desires. Yes, the latter may be pursued, but it escapes no one that depression, suicide or similar events often are more prevalent precisely where improved conditions of material life have been attained.

These observations certainly do not persuade us to renounce any of our desires. Reasonableness alone has never convinced anyone. In fact, in contrast to pre-modern people, once we have satisfied a need we moderns simply move on to the next. In reality our needs have little to do with happiness but much to do with the fact that, having lost faith in transcendent eternity, we look for its surrogate in the infinite prolongation of desire.

Let us close with a little apologue—taken from Tolstoy's *Fables*—which can illustrate the difference between happiness and the satisfaction of needs.

The King and the Nightshirt

A certain king had fallen ill. So he proclaimed, 'I shall give half my kingdom to anyone who can heal me.'
The doctors got together to discuss the matter of a cure. But no one knew what to do. Only one of them came up with an idea: 'We must find a happy man, take his nightshirt from him and put it on the king. That way the king will get well!'

They sent messengers throughout the kingdom in search of a happy man. But the messengers traveled for a long time without finding any. There was no one who was entirely happy. Whoever was rich had some kind of sickness. If by chance someone was healthy and also rich, he had troubles with his wife. Others had wastrels for sons. They all had complaints. One evening the king's son, passing before a cottage, heard a voice saying, 'Thanks be to God! Today I laboured and have my wage, I have eaten and now I am going to sleep. What more do I need?'

The king's son rejoiced and commanded that the nightshirt of that man be brought to him, and that he be given in exchange whatever he wished. The messengers went to the fellow to carry out the order. But that happy man was so poor that he had not even a nightshirt on his back.

As read to the Congress of the Italian Psychological Federation, *On Unhappiness*, Milan, 1991. Published in the acts of the congress, Edizioni UniTor, Rome 1992.

Chapter Seventeen

Analysis and Tragedy

What is analysis? A 'talking cure'? That's hardly an answer. Would a 'talking cure' be a specialised form of therapy (a particular kind of 'cure'), or instead, a specialized form of narrative (a particular kind of 'talking')? In the second case, would it constitute an autonomous form of expression, like poetry or the novel, theatre or the cinema?

The answer to such a question can be highly complex, or extremely direct. At the cost of risking an over-simplification, let us choose the latter course.

The analytic narrative abandons allegiance to the modes of clarity and rationality that hegemonise our times, and the words of the language through which it finds expression are obscure but highly charged, and capable of explaining a great deal more than words that promote clarity while remaining irrelevant to the affects. It constitutes a world of its own. Its codes of expression and its contents belong to itself alone, and they are governed more by principles of drama than by principles of grammar.

Such a genre is quite different from the forms of narrative to which we commonly turn our attention today, and indeed can be seen as their complement; but it is not without precedent. Analysis, as a discipline of knowledge, finds its roots in vast developments that took place in the field of psychiatry in the nineteenth century; but it descends as a form of expression from a much more ancient ancestor: the tradition of tragic narrative.

Rather than any of its heroes or gods, the true protagonist of tragedy is the narrative itself. The tale and its telling are the one true religion to which all of its personages, without exception, pay obeisance.

The characteristics which have always signaled the difference between tragic narrative and the other genres of expression are on the one hand grandly obvious, while also no less mysterious than the meaning of tragedy itself. One notes, for example, that poetry, romance and the novel are stable forms, in the sense that they never die out once having come into existence, whereas tragedy appears and flourishes only in extraordinary epochs, and not even in all such epochs. It clearly finds its nourishment in the spirit that enlivens such times, but one cannot say how. It arises in civilizations which stand at the height of their splendour: in the ancient Greece of Aeschylus, Sophocles and Euripides, in Elizabethan England, in the France of Racine and Corneille, in the Spain of Calderón, and in German Romanticism, but not in the Italian Renaissance.

There is another sense in which tragedy is utterly autonomous: it is not a genre of expression that comes when one calls for it. It is not a continuation of day-to-day forms of expression, and the kinds of questions to which it replies are not conspicuously posed. One cannot sit down at a writing desk, command it to appear, and then proceed to compose it in the way in which a novel, in the final analysis, allows itself to be composed. A novel is the work of its author, whereas tragedy appears to be the work of an invisible tragic spirit. Despite its invisibility, the tragic spirit often assumes the guise of the spirit of a time and a place, or of a *genius loci* which controls and inspires both an author and a public.

Tragedy knows no modesty. It presents itself through great names and in great times, or it doesn't present itself at all. In spite of numberless studies the real reason for such a fact remains a mystery. The very notion of tragedy seems however to laugh at our distress, declaring that tragedy is the celebration of a mystery.

The Christian West—to which we belong even if we are Jews, Muslims or Buddhists—is the most self-critical civilization history has ever known: it is charged not occasionally with discontent, but *always*. This phenomenal sense of permanent discontent concerns analysts no less than historians, and analysts ought to propose explanations for it.

Like Peter after the crowing of the cockerel, the Christian West suffers from feelings of guilt and remorse. Like Peter before that crowing, the Christian West has committed treason. But, unlike Peter, its treason was in no way circumstantial: its treason is synonymous with its very birth.

The West betrayed its Greek cultural roots by joining the revolution that turned it away from myth, mystery and the tragic spirit, impelling it instead towards philosophy and rationalism, as Nietzsche describes throughout his work, but especially in *The Birth of Tragedy*. Additionally, it betrayed its religious roots through the very fact of its adoption of the new faith. The first Christians—whether Jews or pagans, Greeks or Romans—were in any case heretics and apostates: the convert, universally, can know no other destiny.

Treason has therefore remained in the genes of the Christian West, and in its tormented mind, no less than in its blood. Christianity has even insisted on the nature of the act that founded it in its celebration of the anti-religious rites that Dostoyevski describes in his story of the Grand Inquisitor: the Grand Inquisitor condemns the Christ who would hope to return to Earth and supplant the tolerable compromises of the Church with His own intolerable purity (50). This is the source of the Christian image of Judaism as wholly compact and self-consistent: the people and their faith are a single entity, and the faith remains the same throughout the whole of time. As long as the people exist, the faith exists. In this sense, the Christian (even the secular, non-practising Christian) always regards the Jew (even the secular, non-practising Jew) with eyes that are charged with admiration;

and this truth remains unchanged even when admiration lapses into envy, and envy into persecution.

We 'Christians', on the other hand—quotation marks are obligatory, since status as a people is not felt to be enough to define us, and the spirit that might define us has long since taken flight—are always plagued by the knowledge, in some corner of the soul, that we find our origins in those two betrayals: the rejection of the tragic wealth of ancient myth in favour of the simplifications of monotheism; and the rejection of the terrible profundity of Hebraic monotheism in favour of the unilateral goodness of Christianity.

This corner of our souls may also perhaps contain a sense of guilt for having abandoned a view of the world which was much more fearsome, but also, in many ways, more true, since it further corresponds completely to the profound difficulties of living. If this is the case, our discontent can no longer be remedied, since the whole world has grown unilateral, everywhere pursuing this analgesic simplification and this impossible notion of universal goodness. This feeling of culpability finds its manifestation in 'Christian' ethics and education which distance themselves from Christ and revolve around guilt: the sense of guilt is the very foundation on which they have been constructed.

All of this is at odds with psychology. If the presence of guilt in external, practical life is eternal and *inevitable*, what sense can there have been in the introduction of the notion of forgiveness? What sense can it have to free ourselves from the ancient myths, mysteries and sense of tragedy—such enormous treasures of the soul—if instead of creating choice we return to instituting guilt, again denying the soul an original condition of freedom? Can we truly avoid the suspicion that it might indeed have been better to hold to the course of the pre-Christian spirit of Greek pessimism? That spirit, indeed, included guilt, but revolved around its *inevitability*, which in turn forced the individual immediately to come to terms with it. Guilt was a question of destiny, and not of individual responsibility: there was nothing for which to ask to be forgiven, and nothing that inspired a *sense of guilt*, as we understand the term today. Guilt was an inward evil, and an integral part of life, just like external evils. Imprisonment in the category of moral guilt, and in all the self-torture that stems from it, is on the other hand a psychological 'guilt'—a psychological 'sin'—on the part of the Christian insistence on morality, and it reveals the way in which tragedy, nominally dead, continues to guide us along our path. Such invisible 'tragedy' derives from the demise of visible tragedy: one can suppress the literary form, but not the state of pain and laceration which it narrates. That state is a part of the soul's original condition.

The figure of Jehovah, often absurd and implacable as we find him in the Old Testament, still preserves many of the characteristics of the ancient pagan gods: terrible and ambivalent, but profound. With Christianity, such characteristics tended to disappear as the divinity grew more rational, foreseeable, loyal and fair—from human points of view—and one-sidedly good. The merits of Jung also include the distinction of having drawn attention (51) to the fundamentally different ways in which these two different notions of divinity affect the collective mind, both conscious and unconscious; his having couched this perception in terms of an opposition between two peoples, or even between two races, will likewise appear on the list of his major errors.

Christianity—and especially Roman Catholicism, its original and still most widespread form—shows no toleration for opposites that forever intertwine, the one around the other. It tends to resolve them with a unifying synthesis, with a goodness that transcends them, with a dogma, with its election of the image of the shepherd who lifts the burden and torment of choice from the shoulders of his flock. This Christian path—Christian and Cartesian—leads towards rationalization, simplification and peace, even in spite of Christ's admonition, 'Think not that I am come to send peace on earth: I came not to send peace, but a sword' (*Matthew* 10:34). Such a path is in every way similar to the course pursued by the natural sciences with clear and distinct pronouncements of *yes* and *no*, with their fixed and forever-established truths that rout and abolish ambivalence.

Yet the original ambivalence of the inner life finds constant reformulation in life itself, and especially in the ways in which life is experienced by metropolitan humanity, evermore thoroughly abandoned by God, in our complex modern world.

The line of descent from Descartes to the modern individual is not entirely straightforward. After the triumph of the Age of Enlightenment—or indeed of light, *lumière*, in the language of those who invented the Enlightenment—the human individual expected to find him or herself definitively at ease in the world, and as a result to proceed with ever more speed towards rationality and modernity. Instead we were forced to realize that a world made entirely of light, without shadows or *chiaroscuro*, could be a place of enormous suffering. This realization was the prelude to the birth of Romanticism, which appeared with considerable emphasis: a paean to the night as opposed to the day, to irrationality as opposed to reason, to mystery as opposed to knowledge; a rediscovered love for savage nature as opposed to the urban environment, for primitive peoples and their sense of magic as opposed to European needs for a world of predictability. It was likewise rediscovered that the individual consists not only of consciousness, but also of unconsciousness. This perception found its first formation in German Romanticism (in a language with a penchant for depth, and even at times for obscurity, just as the language of Descartes loves clarity and linearity). From there, since this rediscovery of darkness was a moment of great profundity that did not wish to remain confined within the halls of speculation, it descended into the real experience of life, into the world of real ambivalence that continues to torture our nights, in spite of the lives we live by day. It is here that we discover the birth of psychoanalysis.

The manifesto of this new perception of complexity was Faust's exclamation: *Du bist dir nur des einen Trieb bewusst, / O lerne nei den andern kennen! / Zwei Seelen wohnen, ach! In meiner Brust / Die eine will sich von der andern trennen* ('You are aware of but a single drive, / And may you never know the other! / Two souls, ah! live within my breast / The one would take its distance from the other' (*Faust*, Part I, 'Vor dem Tor' 1.111-13).

Bleuler lifted the Faustian split from the complex world of poetic imagery and transformed it into a psychiatric concept, inaugurating the use of the notion of ambivalence (52). Psychoanalysis was an essential part of this general cultural revival, especially in the case of Jung, who was Bleuler's major student at the Burghölzli.

It is said that those who do not know their history do not know themselves; and if we analysts are less than clearly aware of belonging to this great historical current of thought that turns new attention to the soul, we too might be accused of an insufficient knowledge of ourselves and of our profession.

So, psychoanalysis had to be invented in order once again to give a space to obscurity and profundity. These are things of which the modern man would no longer like to have bear the burden, but they check his every intention to throw them off, and doggedly continue to pursue him. Psychoanalysis had to be invented in order to reconstruct a place where mystery once more might be a sacred guest rather than always an enemy, always to be slain.

The obscurity, depth and complexity which our souls can never definitively resolve find manifestation not only in the terms of Bleuler's notion of ambivalence, but also in the two forms of thought described by Jung (53). Basically, morality, law, science, politics and a large area of philosophy are all concerned with the part of us that shapes clear thoughts, and which is gifted with the faculty of choice. Analysis, on the other hand, is left almost entirely alone—even religion is more than content to desert its field—with everything within us that is paralysed by ambivalence, hypnotized by mystery, and fearfully immersed in eternal contemplation of the uselessness of all the greatest efforts of the will. This portion of us is far from small or insignificant. Most of us seem indeed to pass directly from a womb to a tomb with few clear thoughts in between, and never having chosen anything for ourselves. Most of the few of us who exercise some faculty of choice in the course of our lives seem only to do so at crucial moments.

Ambivalence is the rule of the way our psyche functions; whereas choosing and taking a stand on things constitute the exception, an exception that finds its birth in very great pain. So ambivalence is the original condition, still mantled with primal confusion; and Freud quite justly noted that ambivalence grows increasingly stronger as we shift our eyes to the individuals of ever more primitive cultures (54). The frame of mind and the narrative form which directed their attention to this far from tiny part of the human being were referred to as tragic. We find their beginnings in ancient epic and their first culmination in the Greek tragedies, true and proper.

The tragic spirit sees the human being, from a moral point of view, as an inseparable mixture of good and evil—not good and evil by turns as a result of some conversion, but always both, at one and the same time. In terms of will and the drawing of mental distinctions, the human being is eternally trapped in ambivalence: we desire a thing and its opposite not in successive moments, with one desire supplanting the other owning to a change of ideas, but simultaneously.

Since the era of classical antiquity, tragedy has suddenly reappeared in various epochs. Yet on the whole, it receded to an ever greater distance in the course of history, and was finally abandoned in favour of more modern and optimistic forms of narrative. The tragic spirit was deposed to make room for other attitudes, increasingly influenced by science, which was assuming evermore importance and taking the place of religion; these newer attitudes were therefore much more positive and more concerned with objective fact. But since the human being continued all the same to experience ambivalence, we found ourselves with the need, in the very midst of the modern age, to invent a new form of narrative through which to give expression to ambivalence. This is why analysis was invented: for the purpose of providing a cure for the unilateral modes of expression that typified the modern age, and not for the purpose of providing a cure for psychic disturbances which had always existed.

When we take a close look at the tragic myth of Oedipus, we have to conclude that the great discoveries of Sigmund Freud have little to with this hero. As I attempted to show in a former publication (55), the hero of Sophocles' *Oedipus Rex* is not afflicted by a sexual problem, but by a problem of knowledge. Oedipus wants to know his origins, as would surely be natural in any epoch. Yet he lacked a likewise natural respect—natural at the time of Sophocles—for the residue of mystery that lies around the question of origin, no less than around the question of the final purposes of life: a residue of mystery which rational thought can never eliminate. Oedipus attempted to apply the abilities of a modern police detective to the task of the reconstruction and clarification of all the events connected with his birth. Instead, he made the acquaintance of the mystery and tragedy that lie behind every human life; the drama tells us quite literally that blindness, rather than clarity, lay at the end of his path.

We are finally faced with the kind of victory that a tragic destiny typically achieves, with all its derision of the trivial human will. To understand the drama of Oedipus we have to understand this logic, and we must attempt to remain within it, accepting its internal completeness and total self-consistency. If we imagine, for example, that blindness was a punishment for an error on the part of Oedipus, we have already missed the mark and entered the sphere of a much more modern logic: the logic of Christian morality, and of the scientific notion that effects are always provoked by causes. But the triumph of blindness in this case is the triumph of the realm of mystery. At the beginning of *Oedipus Rex*, only Tiresias, the wise man, is blind: blind and limited. At the end, Oedipus too is blind, who had previously derided Tiresias, calling him the seer who could not see. Oedipus has reached and accepted the limits of knowledge, and they have brought him to a form of natural wisdom.

Those who struggle for clarity alone—as in the case of Oedipus, the hero of rationality—finally turn out to be more exhausted voyagers, since they are always even more distant from a port: every clarification brings the formerly unsuspected need for another in its wake. Those, instead, who accept the realm of mystery are like a sailor who has reached a shore: it is fearful and dark, but land lies solid beneath his feet.

Tragedy insisted that the human being, even when we think ourselves to be exercising the faculty of choice, is only a tiny instrument in the hands of destiny, just as analysis teaches that the human ego is basically only a tiny instrument in the hands of unconscious forces. Tragedy couches this statement not only by way of its contents, but also by way of the fact of its very existence or non-existence, in the sense that its manifestation is not determined by its author. Just as tragedy, unlike other narrative forms, is independent of its author and controlled by a tragic spirit far too profound to be identified, in much the same way analysis, unlike traditional medical therapies, is not controlled by the therapist, but by forces too unconscious to be truly guided. Like destiny again, such unconscious forces (we prefer to use 'unconscious' as an adjective, since we don't want to formulate a metaphysics, but only to describe the desperate limitations of our forms of knowledge) use all the facets of ambivalence, and all the daily manifestations of tragic impotence, as tolls with which to guide our lives, revealing such things to supplant us, and leading us to face the fact that they are vastly more powerful than we are.

The moments when we imagine ourselves to be in the act of making a choice are often, in fact, the very same moments when we are smallest, weakest and most entirely damned. We imagine our mental clarity to have vanquished the human passions, but in fact remain in the grip of the most treacherous passion of all: *hýbris* (56), the arrogance that makes us blind, or, more precisely, that which makes us incapable of perceiving the proportions and limits of everything human. *Hýbris*, moreover, is the only sin which is common to all religions. It is also the only sin which is common to every epoch: a sin both religious and secular, natural and cultural, ancient and modern. It is the sin of pride for Jews and Christians, the sin of the illusion of action for Buddhists. It is the endless multiplication of needs which offends the laws of nature; and it is the arrogance of the individual which offends the laws of society. The ancients saw it as a sin against the equilibrium of nature; in the modern age it is a sin against the principles of psychic equilibrium (the *hýbris* of consciousness, the absurd and pretentious demand that everything which takes place in the psyche be conscious and free from mystery [57]). This final sin closes the circle, bringing us back to antiquity, since Oedipus suffered from a cognitive arrogance of precisely such a nature.

With its condemnation of *hýbris*, tragedy had already taken up the task of teaching a form of modesty that corresponds to what modern psychoanalysis refers to as the reality principle. *Hýbris* is the insolent conviction that one can deal as one sees fit with the laws of destiny and the forces of the psyche. It is the arrogance of the man who believes himself able to substitute himself for God, either in the governance of the inner world, since he decides to guide the emotions with the will, and accordingly to control the autonomous life of the soul, or in the governance of the outer world, since he takes on the part of God in the administration of the truth, and often, of life and death. The incredulous horror inspired by the acts of political terrorists lie less in the sight of so much blood than in the sight of their omnipotent stupidity. Whenever an assassin has thought himself able to reach a rational decision on how best to change the course of history, he has instead unleashed an unforeseeable series of passions of infinitely greater complexity than the workings of his simple intellect.

In general, *hýbris* is the naivety of the person who pursues his courses of action in an attitude of idolatry for his own decisions. The vast mistrust with which most of the Western world regards its politicians has less to do with disinterest, or with preferences for other politicians, than with a feeling of diffidence for all the incurable *hýbris* of people who wield power.

Our times present us with still another paradox. As a form of narration, tragedy has disappeared. However, the tragic narrative found its subject in *hýbris,* and presented a parable on the ruin and uselessness of arrogance. *Hýbris* today is more widespread than ever.

How is all of this reflected in analysis? 'How' is difficult to say. Yet it is reflected constantly. Analysis might be defined as an attempt to become more conscious through a continuous act of self-criticism: a slow labour of deconstruction on all the ingenuous attitudes of omnipotence that we carry within ourselves. But a constantly growing consciousness can itself be tempted by omnipotence, like the frog that mistakes itself for a bull.

The analyst sails between Scylla and Charybdis; the patient is plagued by a lack of self-confidence and the analyst has to help the patient to put on the brakes when he or she is possessed by the frenzy of consciousness, by the arrogance of analysis for the sake of analysis. The analyst has to remind the patient, as it is put in the New Testament, that 'whoever shall exalt himself shall be abased; and he that shall humble himself shall be exalted' (*Matthew* 23:12, *Luke* 18:14, etc.).

It is precisely here, however, that we find the greatest danger, for the analyst as well as for the patient. The analyst has to speak like the Gospel whist remaining clearly aware that his or the words used are not Gospel. So, *hýbris* is a hidden and ever-present danger for the analyst as well. This holds true not only for the analyst as an individual, but also for the whole of analytic theory. It is enough to look back at some of the words which were written by various masters in the 1960s and 1970s, at a time when they were ready to declare that the diffusion of analysis, in association with the revolution for a more just society, would promote a kind of general psychic hygiene. We read these words today and recognize the *hýbris* of a mode of positive thinking which saw itself on the road to a happy ending that would take the form of a universal adventure in psychotherapy. Yet our language may now have grown more refined, but with little change in substance. Even the titles of a number of the books which criticize the *hýbris* of our times might be cited as examples: *We've Had a Hundred Years of Psychotherapy and the World's Getting Worse* (58). Whoever said it was going to get better? Who, if not anti-tragic *hýbris*, which analysis itself should combat?

Guilt is a universal presence, but it does not explain everything. The great fascination with which North Americans look back at the history of the Native American peoples cannot, for example, be explained as exclusively a question of feelings of guilt for the genocidal wars of the past, nor indeed as a question of the current need to adhere to politically correct ideologies. If that were the case, it would be enough to rewrite history from the point of view of the vanquished and to actuate programmes for the rehabilitation of those marginal niches of society in which they now find refuge. Yet the realization of such ideas on even the vastest of scales would not assuage the American hunger for the culture of the North American Indians. America's fascination with its native peoples goes far beyond anything objective, concrete and rational, and is also a great deal more than a feeling of anxiety with respect to the discovery of roots, given that the quantity of Native American blood which flows through the veins of the rest of the people on the North American continent is a good deal lower than the percentage of alcohol that is permitted in the veins of a person at the wheel of a car, and that the very name America is Florentine.

There is a very simple way of explaining this situation. The guiding force of the Western world- America-has also invented the form of narrative that dominates it. Hollywood has written the codes that control modern narrative and thereby has established the nature of the modern hero: we are presented with men and women who choose, who align themselves with the powers of goodness, who entrust its redemption to willful action, and who never doubt its final triumph. It cannot be said that this form of narrative is necessarily inferior to others, but it can be said to show an anti-tragic one-sidedness. It sanctions the disappearance of tragedy from the language of our times.

In the great panoramas of American history, one does not have to go very far afield—either in space or time—to discover a redress for this partial and one-sided view of things. The discourses of Chief Joseph of the Nez Percé, of His Crazy Horse and of every other Indian Chief give us precisely that vision which is most conspicuously absent from America's narratives on the triumph of positive, human will, and indeed, more generally, from the whole of the modern, developed world: the vision of tragic dignity. The Hollywood hero strives for justice when his rights have been offended; the Indian Chief knows that life is the seat of drama, not of justice, and prepares himself in all tranquility for the next blow of destiny. The Hollywood hero fights a battle which he fully intends to win, a battle that the Indian Chief knows can only postpone defeat. The Hollywood hero believes in the supreme power of will; the Indian Chief, like the tragic hero, believes that will counts for nothing, even if none the less it has to follow its course. It has to follow its path as a part of the plans drawn up by destiny, and not at all by virtue of the worth of any plans he has made. The Hollywood hero is ingenuous; the Indian Chief is wise. America's thirst for the narratives of the continent's native peoples asserts itself so powerfully because the narratives of the dominant culture are so thoroughly unilateral. They present themselves as unilateral not only from historical points of view but also, or indeed primarily, from the point of view of the spirit.

Therefore, America's need to lend an ear to the voices of its 'primitive' peoples is more than an historical necessity; it also corresponds to a psychological need of American collective consciousness, or, more generally, of the modern collective conscience. And what about the psychological needs of the modern individual consciousness? We can point to a situation which is absolutely parallel. The will is an insufficient tool for confronting obstacles within life. It is often to be noted that highly willful individuals are precisely the people who are most prone to encounter a state of psychic paralysis: they find themselves blocked not by external circumstances, but by interior ones. The modern individual becomes aware of desiring opposite things at one and the same time, and he or she also realizes that such a situation is more than a question of some specific snag in a given and specific circumstance: it presents itself instead as a kind of 'natural' and permanent condition, as a condition that corresponds to the rediscovery of the deep psyche and of all the ambivalence that riddles it.

The most expected solution to this 'natural obstacle' is to take the problem to an adequately trained professional, who goes by the name of the analyst. It is not, however, that the natural thing is to accord so high a level of trust to this professional; as a rule one will not know this person, or not in any personal way, and one's attitude of trust is self-imposed: a self-imposed faith in the general, modern notion of technical proficiency and specialization, and, as well, it is once again the product of an act of will. The natural thing is the inclination to recount one's torments, and the faith that it serves some purpose to do so. What is archetypal is the faith in narration. The narration of ambivalence is the rediscovery—unconsciously, and in ways which are therapeutic and individual—of the tradition of the narration of pain: the tradition of the tragic narrative.

So, it is not at all by chance that analysis has spread so widely in the twentieth century—'the American Century'(59). It is not because our epoch is necessarily more neurotic than those that preceded it. Morevoer it is because our epoch, like every other, needs narration (60). Since our century's controlling emblems are those which find their extremes in the anthropology of Hollywood, our century's conscious values are afflicted by much the same forms of optimistic insistence on the power of human will, and by the same anti-tragic one-sidedness. To compensate for this unilateralism, the people of North America, and indeed of the whole of the modern world, have given great space, in their cultural lives, to the narratives of so-called primitive peoples; and the same compensation, in their private lives, is supplied by the narrative of analysis.

When the mass media tell us that economic and social conditions are preparing to give us a tragic future—which is something one hears quite frequently here in Italy—they intuit something central, but turn the problem upside-down. It is not that social and economic problems will give us the feeling of living in a tragic world, but rather that the lack of tragic feeling will remove all sense from an economy and society which in any case is by far the most sated that history has known.

The ancient Greeks thus invented the basic narrative of the Western world: we can take the epics and tragedies as a single, unified entity, and refer to it as the tragic narrative.

The Greeks believed that life is the briefest of moments, whereas the narrative that tells its tale is eternal. So, the narrative of life is superior to life itself. Not even our modern experience—grounded in omnipotent individualism—can contradict that feeling. It is clear that we have lost all access to the myths of origin from which the Greeks derived the plots and actions of tragic narrative, and that we no longer have any knowledge of the state in which we existed before our birth, just as we no longer know what will happen to us after we die. But in spite of this (and indeed precisely because of this) narrative remains, for modern humanity as well, the more important experience, for indeed it remains central.

The mind's need for the eternal by no means disappears, nor even diminishes, with the lapse of all discourse on eternal things—with the loss of myth, of religion and of metaphysics—in the world that lies around the mind. The contemplation of eternity no longer finds its home in a glorious collective tradition, but in narrative accounts of ordinary, individual experience, as in Camus' *L'Étranger*, or Joyce's *Ulysses*. For people who belong to the modern world, true narrative has to spring up out of life: it is found in the instant that transcends itself and makes itself eternal, which expresses not chance but meaning, and even—and this is more than a game with words—the meaning of chance. Existentialism too sees narrative as a place of refuge from daily life. Our minds are committed to secular thought, or to secular points of view, and we no longer attempt to turn narrative into the seat of religious belief. But we unfailingly— archetypally?—continue to believe in narration (61). Hence, a psychotherapeutic cure seems to us to be good and convincing when it takes on the structure of a well-told tale. But we should also see that this is modern-centric prejudice. It is not that the cure assumes the guise of narrative, but rather that the act of narration assumes the guise of a cure.

We can see the tragic narrative as having conserved its own autonomy, as having asked to be reinvented. The tragic tale was invented in ages that long preceded psychotherapy, and already at its time of origin it sought to serve the very same purpose which its rediscovery was to posit for itself in the course of the last century: not pleasure, but meaning.

In order to exit from meaninglessness and pain, human beings have always come together around a fire and a story-teller, no less in Homer's Greece than among the tribes of all the world's five continents. Homer, however, achieved eternal renown by virtue of the fact that someone, one day, wrote down his stories. Since that time, the story of the events that Homer relates moves us just as much as the events themselves, indeed somewhat more. Homer's immortality lies in his having formulated this one fundamental statement: that important facts come about for the purpose of being narrated. The gods desired the destruction of Troy in order that the tale might be told (*Odyssey* VIII.579-80). Odysseus, who could hold back tears while watching the suffering and death of persons he loved, didn't know how to hold them back *while listening to the tale of his own adventures* (*Odyssey* VIII.86-8, 522-31). The protagonists of the Trojan War cannot avoid pain, nor indeed would they have dreamed of doing so: what they see as important, and as filling their actions with meaning, is the fact that their actions will later be recounted (*Iliad* VI.358).

Do we analysts really do anything much different from that? Analysis appears to restore a sense of life to the individual insofar as it rearranges the events of the individual's life and gives them an order which in fact is both narrative and creative, rather than interpretative (62). The analytic setting is just a little less strait than solitude: two of you sit beside the fire. Experience has taught us that the transformation of pain is due far less to its medication on the part of an external force, than to the activation of an internal force that can organize it into a narrative. If the narrative of life is superior to life itself, pain too is of lesser moment than the narrative of pain.

Notions of happy endings forget the wisdom that comes from antiquity, just as they forget the lessons that come from the experience of analysis itself. All their attention is simply directed to the attempt to overcome pain. This, perhaps, is the most dramatic of the many forms of repression that typify our times: it amounts, in fact, to the repression of all sense of drama. One wonders if the next millennium will be a millennium that knows no tragic sentiment.

As Nietzsche reminds us, the birth of philosophy, or, better, the appearance of Socrates, also occasioned the birth of the optimism of the will: philosophy opened the road to science and rationality, and to the disappearance of depth and mystery in a sated and utterly secular world.

Even if constructed on the basis of a pre-Enlightenment, and largely pre-Socratic logic, which preferred the individual sage to abstract wisdom, analysis is an obviously modern phenomenon. Yet analysis, rather than philosophy, presents itself as the true heir of tragedy. Analysis marks the return of the cult of repressed Dionysus, the ambiguous god, the ambivalent god, the god of the indissoluble dualism of the good and evil in the clay from which God moulded us, the god of the inalterability of destiny, which lives within me, just as God, the soul and the unconscious live within me. True analysis is undertaken in the tragic spirit and with tragic decision, and not in the medical spirit that insistently wants to heal, while lending no attention to the soul. One faces up to analysis in order to nurture oneself on that personal piece of destiny which Jungian jargon refers to as individuation.

The sense of belonging that derives from recognizing a destiny as 'one's own' doesn't necessarily lead to a healing. However, it leads to the experience of a 'metaphysical consolation' not dissimilar to the consolation which Nietzsche saw as inherent to tragedy (63). The story of a life is tantamount to the rediscovery of the sense of self which makes us who and what we are, precisely by virtue of being the progeny of just that story—that story, that history, those precise roots—and not of any other (64).

Analysis hinges on the experience of interminable paradox, as well as on the experience of ambivalence and contradiction as events that do not wholly define me, but which nonetheless give me an identity. If this is analysis—and certainly analysis is *also* this—it stands at a very great distance from the optimism of Socratic-medical thinking.

Secret affinities can act as a bridge between phenomena which belong to vastly different times, and which a superficial view of history would see as quite separate from one another. Tragedy and analysis, on the one hand, are related to one another, just as philosophy and medicine on the other. The first pair respects the inherent ambivalence of human experience: the common model of tragedy and analysis shows great regard for the mystery of life and makes no attempt to turn the world into an image of the ego, accepting the fully self-evident fact that the world precedes the ego. Conversely, philosophy and medicine, on the other hand, share a univalent tendency that thinks in terms of finalities, and of the value of human will.

Analysis therefore presents itself as one of the very few antidotes to modern *hýbris*: to the temptations of the search for ever greater power—the power to do—and of the tendency to confront all problems with the thought of being able to solve them. The patient's goal does not lie in achieving the ability *to do* something new (which, at best, is the specific characteristic of brief therapies that aim for specific results). The patient's goal is *to be*; even at the times when nothing, or nearly nothing, is the only thing that he or she can do.

One might wonder if these reflections on tragedy can be of any help to the actual, day-to-day practice of analysis with actual specific patients. I believe they can be. It is usual for practicing analysts already to be quite accustomed to showing a great respect for their patients' moments of 'drama'—for their patients' most painful experiences and for the moments and ways in which their patients present them. These are moments in which the analyst is likely to be in the habit of postponing interpretation: instinctively, since our feelings tell us that interpretative intervention would interrupt the patient's narrative. We know that the narrative, in moments like these, has to take precedence over everything else. Yet if we see the model of the analyst's work in the light of a 'tragic model', the ancestor to which it runs parallel, we can help the analyst understand the reasons for such actions.

This kind of behaviour does not spring up by chance or in that particular moment: it is a fruit of the very same tree that once produced tragedy.

On a private and individual plane, analysis can again call up that tragic split which, in great, crucial and very special moments, has taken hold of the whole of certain cultures. History, in fact, makes it clear that tragedy can never be the permanent, ordinary mode of expression through which a culture speaks. When ordinary times return, tragedy disappears, and then shows a tendency to reappear in subsequent moments of transformation and creativity (65).

Doesn't something similar happen with the individual? When patients subject themselves to permanent analysis, their enthusiasm wanes: they turn into bureaucrats of the unconscious. Patients, on the other hand, who do not turn analysis into a permanent undertaking—a programme for the unconscious—are able to return to it at the proper time; they are able to resume analysis when a new period of transformation autonomously presents itself, more than in the wake of any sort of plan. Essentially, this is no different from the sort of discussion we table when we reflect on a patient's motivation, and on the importance of careful assessment, both at the start of analysis and repeatedly as events progress. Patients who undertake analysis because analysis has been prescribed, or on the basis of intentions simply to exploit its techniques, and who do so with no deep passion, have limited possibilities of success. In any case, chances of success are a great deal higher for patients who enter analysis for fortuitous or circumstantial reasons without really understanding why, but who nevertheless recount their stories with desperate enthusiasm. This would seem to be a paradox. However, it is actually the equivalent to saying that the first model, the model of the medical cure, is less appropriate to analysis than that of the tragic narrative; the courage to exist within paradox was in fact the kind of courage that typified the tragic hero.

Every patient who goes to the bottom of what we call the confrontation with the shadow has something in common with the evil heroes to which tragedy has accustomed us. These sorts of hero (Medea, Macbeth) can indeed see the evil within which they are involved, but they look on in amazement at the powerful perversion that holds them in its tow. They no longer understand themselves nor why they have to act out this torment. They know themselves to be two things at the very same time, and yet they also know that their ambivalence will not prevent them from acting. It is not that Medea murders her sons because she does not love them; she murders her sons in spite of the fact that she loves them.

The Hollywood villain has lost this sort of human complexity, and to live in the Hollywood era means no longer to have any models for our lacerating conflicts, for our confrontation with the shadow. To rediscover the tragic spirit, we are forced to make it over into 'the century of analysis'. If we succeed we will finally obey our passions; and perhaps we will also discover the depths of such a well of obedience that offers a redemption more profound than any hardly credible, sudden and utterly intentional change in our behaviour. Like the tragic hero, a patient is likely to feel that the conviction of being able suddenly to change for the better can conceal no small amount of *hýbris*: the arrogance, for tragedy, of those who desire to alter their destiny, and the arrogance, for analysis, of those who desire, immediately and at any cost, to impose consciousness on the unconscious.

If the patient is to be a tragic hero, the analyst too has to have the ability to respect the patient's status as such. In precisely those moments to which we refer, significantly enough, as 'dramatic', the analyst's task is not to interpret the patient, but to observe the patient in much the same way that a viewer observes a tragic drama: in a spirit of respect for the greatness of the character—all of us ought to have our own particular greatness—and in a spirit of participation, free of all preconceived theories, with respect to the actions of that character. Like the appearance of the truly tragic denouement, the appearance of the moment of truth in analysis—and this is the manifestation of true analysis—is frequently not theorisable, nor foreseeable, because it is not concept but vision: only later can we deal with it on any such terms, after the drama has found its consummation.

The patient who enters analysis brings along two things which are always highly personal: a personal narrative and a personal pain. Both are unique and cannot belong, or be made to belong, to anyone else. The analysis, indeed, might be mortally wounded if the analyst were to tell the patient that this particular narrative and this particular pain were anything other than totally unique. Just as the narrative and the pain are tied together by a knot that cannot be undone, they are likewise tied, by a similar knot, to the patient's individuality. This particular suffering and this particular narrative are things that this particular patient cannot, and must not, forget. The novelty which the narrative is able to produce is meaning. The narrative can redirect the energy and the gaze which before bent only backwards—towards the torments of the patient's fragmented past—and project them into a continuity that gives them a painful place in a unified train of events which also includes a life that moves on into the future.

Christianity espouses values which are no less affirmative than those of science, and is always opposed to death. Analysis, on the other hand, like tragedy, is mysterious, problematic and ambivalent, and interrogates itself on the goal of life without knowing a reply from the start. The analyst knows that he cannot always voice an objection— always, and in any case, and with all possible force—to the patient who talks about suicide (66); such words can be a necessary chapter of the patient's narrative. Here again, and additionally without being conscious of it, the analyst, finally, has invented no new vision of his own, but instead has rediscovered the classical attitude: it is an attitude that includes the tragic code which insisted, unlike Christianity, that the ultimate moment, that of a choice in the face of death, was profoundly personal and had to be respected. It was less a question of addressing a choice than of sounding an inscrutable link between the individual and his or her destiny.

The profound relationship between the models of analysis and tragedy—and their common distance from the medical model—tell us why the analyst can be no constant partisan of an always inflexible defence of life. The analyst must indeed be passionately allied with the patient—with the patient's well-being, with the patient's life, and even, at the final extreme, with the patient's death—but paradoxically (and we know by now that paradox is a confirmation, not a contradiction, of the tragic spirit) the analyst has to control that passion. Freud too—despite his commitment to a medical model, and notwithstanding his lack of all use for the concept of individuation—was already thinking this thought when he counseled the therapist (67) to avoid any over-intense desire to heal, adding as well that one should not make too many plans in the course of any healing. We have reason to remember that Freud's profound experience in analytic technique was accompanied by a thorough knowledge of the Greek tragedies. The tragic myth gave warning that blindness was the lot of precisely the person who had wanted to see too much, and Freud may perhaps have taken those words more seriously than we imagine.

We are familiar with the notion of the action which aims to achieve a goal and which hopes to procure a good, since it belongs not only to the positive thinking of the medical frame of mind, but also, from much further back in antiquity, to the Hebrew and Christian frame of mind. The torment of Job was terrible, but we cannot call it tragic, since it reflected the will of God and was an instrument of God's justice (68). The notion of justice, and of establishing justice, is the factor that sets up the absolute difference between the attitudes, on the one hand, of science and religion, and, on the other, of tragedy—as well, as I see it, of analysis. The sufferings of the patient do not, in fact, present themselves, in their very own right, as 'just' or 'unjust'; neither do they belong to a divine plan for the final establishment of justice. It is true that they may acquire a meaning some day, but they can also remain a meaningless waste. The only thing certain in this instance is that a narrative account of these sufferings can be composed and listened to. The ideal analytic experience suspends intentions without suspending emotions, on the part of the patient no less than on the part of the analyst, and what results is a kind of pure emotion. But this, precisely, is the way in which tragic emotion would be described. James Joyce describes it thus:

> *The tragic emotion…is a face looking two ways, towards terror and towards pity, both of which are phases of it.* [He wrote a few lines earlier that 'Pity is the feeling which arrests the mind in the presence of whatsoever is grave and constant in human sufferings and unites it with the secret cause'. He continues;] *You see I use the word arrest. I mean that the tragic emotion is static. . . The feelings excited by improper art are kinetic, desire or loathing. Desire urges us to possess, to go to something; loathing urges us to abandon, to go from something. These are kinetic emotions. . . The [tragic] emotion. . . is. . . static. The mind is arrested and raised above desire and loathing (69).*

First published in Ann Casement, ed., *Post-Jungians Today*. Routledge, London, 1998, chapter 2, pp. 33-49.

(50) Fyodor Dostoyevski, *The Brothers Karamazov*. (1879-80)V.5.
(51) C.G. Jung, *Answer to Job* (1952). *Collected Works*, vol. 11.
(52) Eugen Bleuler, *Lehrbuch der Psychiatrie*. Berlin, Springer, 1955, Part II.3.I. Bleuler intuits the essence of ambivalence when he speaks of it as an *intimate, tragic laceration*. He seems, however, to go astray and to speak in reductive terms when in his attempt to establish psychiatric classifications he sees it as the basis of a disturbance of the mental functions. Ambivalence should instead be recognized as the normal and fundamental basis on which the psyche operates.

(53) C.G. Jung, *Symbols of Transformation* (1912/1952). *Collected Works* vol. 5, Part I, Chapter 2.
(54) Sigmund Freud, *Totem and Taboo* (1912-13). Standard Edition XIII, chapter 2.
(55) *La Pratica Analitica*, vol.10 - no.11, 1995.
(56) I dealt with this argument in *Growth and Guilt*. Routledge, London and New York, 1995.
(57) C.G. Jung, *Psychology and Religion* (1940). CW 11.
(58) James Hillman and M. Ventura (1993).
(59) See G. Alvi, *Il secolo americano*. Milan, Adelphi, 1966.
(60) See also B. Reale, *Le macchie di Leonardo*. Bergamo, Moretti & Vitali, 1998.
(61) Studies of serial killers have revealed that a number of such individuals have consciously chosen to consign themselves to life imprisonment or to death by execution rather than to live out the intolerable suffering of a life so anonymous that it could never be recounted. (I owe this information to a still unpublished essay by Carole Beebe Tarantelli.)
(62) Aniela Jaffé, *The Myth of Meaning*, Zurich, Bollingen, 1967/70.
(63) Friedrich Nietzsche, *The Birth of Tragedy* (1872/1972). Chapter 17.
(64) The notable success of an apparently small-scale book like *Power in the Helping Professions*, by Adolf Guggenbühl-Craig (New York, Spring, 1971) lies precisely in the tragic spirit—charged with emotional participation but free from all laments—with which it describes the inevitability of the presence of the shadow in analysis, which in spite of this, and indeed for precisely this reason, preserves its meaning.
(65) George Steiner, *The Death of Tragedy* (1961). See especially Chapter 4.
(66) James Hillman, *Suicide and the Soul*. New York, Harper and Row, 1964.
(67) For example, in 'Ratschläge für den Artzt bei der Psychanalytischen Behandlung', in *Zur Technik der Psychanalyse* (1911-12), Standard Edition XII.
(68) Steiner, *op.cit*, Chapter 1.
(69) James Joyce, *A Portrait of the Artist as a Young Man* (1914-15). Harmondsworth, Penguin, 1971, p. 204.

Chapter Eighteen

In Praise of Not Choosing

What do the death of Lady Diana and a recent congress of the Federation of Italian Psychologists have in common? The congress had 'choice' as its theme, a problem that concerns both Lady Diana Spencer and ourselves.

In a long 'cultural necrology', Alice Schwarzer has said that the princess did not know how to make choices (*Die Zeit* 37, 1997; Ms Schwarzer is a leading German feminist). Was she today's woman or yesterday's? She was both subject and object. She knew how to shatter the most established conventions, but not how to go her own way. She knew how to impress men but remained their tool, for dynastic purposes or those of social promotion, indifferently. This way of being made her no less interesting and no less comprehensible. On the contrary, it made her real: human. She offered a container for the widest array of projections from the broadest sort of public. Women from the most diverse class backgrounds and nationalities, and men as well, were able to identify with her.

Taking a leaf from this brief analysis, we can call Lady Diana's myth 'the myth of not choosing'. The myth of choice is a cultural value minted quite recently, a credo that began to flesh itself out in the Enlightenment, but which only in this century has become truly part of a system of shared collective values: the *American way of life*. This notion of lifestyle has spread throughout Europe only in the last half century, and, in the last few years, to all those other countries affected by globalization. The myth, so-called, consists of the presupposition that everyone has either the right to make or the possibility of making choices concerning their own life, and that these occasions present themselves every day. It is a theoretical notion, a scheme far from being a concrete thing or a profound emotion (a genuine myth) for most of us (and for this reason it would be better to speak about an 'ideology' of choice).

It is abstract because the difficulty of choice concerns everyone. In reality, the incapacity to make choices represents a normal condition. The illusion that we may continually exercise choice is instead an extraordinary revolution, which has been carried out in the last few decades under our very eyes almost without anyone noticing.

Let us take account of what this myth is not. The fish of choice seem to be winning out because they have discovered a limitless sea through which to swim in the business economy. The great supermarket in which we live leads us to think that we are always making choices. Like the state, it proclaims the right to be healthy and promises lots of aspirin but does nothing to impede the growth of cancer, just as the global economy talks about the right to choose whilst restricting it to drinking either Coca Cola or Pepsi. Our freedom of choice grows while we almost never choose the really important things, limited as we are to ratifying what external circumstances have decided. This is so even in the case of love, as the soaring divorce rate demonstrates; divorce has been tapped rather late in the game to remedy this deficiency.

How have we been made so credulous as to believe in the possibility of endless choice? The ideology of choice, in order to become more than an abstract code, to become a myth, also has needed to have an image of choice, a hero, and to spread that image through channels of communication so that it becomes popular, but not real. The instrument of popularization has been the global spectacle, the world of Hollywood. Hollywood heroes do not stand out because they are strong; Homer's heroes have already represented this. Additionally, they do not stand out because they are pure in heart, for they have that in common with the medieval sagas and romances. The Hollywood hero is conspicuous in that he makes choices and unfailingly carries on: an image already mainstream, indeed planetary in scope, victorious through sheer numbers. Yet also an image of someone who has never existed and in whom it is difficult to believe. A one-sided image wholly lacking in depth, which comes with the Hollywood name, whilst retaining the faintest hint of superciliousness.

As we have said (70), if we limit ourselves to essentials, images of the human come down to only two. One is classical, the other is Hollywood. One is the man of paradox, of contradiction and ambivalence. The other is the man of choice or decision. One is the natural subject, the other is not. The man described by the classical tradition is the figure of tragedy, ancient epic, of scripture and the great literature of every age. He always has weight and depth; often he surveys the evil in which he finds himself so as to plunge into it and hopefully to avoid it. Nearly always, however, he finds that he has no choice. Orestes knows that if he kills Clytemnestra he will stand condemned as a matricide; should he not kill her, he will live in shame as a son who failed to avenge his father. All the same, he must get on with his own destiny and fully live out to its end his own contradiction.

His is no special case of a passionate character indifferent to self-discipline. The same thing befell Saint Paul, who said, 'I do not do the good I want, but the evil I do not want is what I do' (*Romans* 7.19). Paul is the grand strategist who made Christianity a success with the masses, but from our point of view he is the hero of contradictions, once again a subspecies of the tragic hero.

This paralysis in the tragic figure hardly saves the heroes of Shakespeare. These figures, once again, know how to act but not how to choose: not only the ambivalent Hamlet but also the daring Macbeth, who lucidly assesses the right way of behaving in his situation and rejects it. As is always the case with the tragic hero, destiny and passion prove stronger than clarity of mind; it is arrogant to oppose these powers, where it is right to become putty in their hands and let them mould one's character. Macbeth is the hero in his drama not because he chooses evil, but on the contrary because he cannot do otherwise.

At the doorway to modernity stands Faust. Goethe's hero has will, which is the precondition for choice. Unfortunately, it is anything but a unified will: 'Two souls', we hear him cry, 'live in my breast'. Much more than to external struggles Faust is pledged to the ones that continue within him.

After undoing the unity of the will, Nietzsche also dismantles the unity of consciousness: 'A thought comes', he says, 'when 'it' wishes to and not when 'I' want it to' (*Beyond Good and Evil*, I.17). Psychoanalysis appropriates this 'it' and installs it at the center of a system that speaks pessimistically about human freedom. It has sent out into our time the unsung heroes of the interior struggle: patients in analysis. They succeed in finding healing not, as the stereotype has it, by coming to know the causes of their suffering, but by successfully entering into the truth of a story which has nothing to do with Hollywood.

Why enlarge consciousness but not the faculty of choice? Because consciousness is above all the awareness of that which does not exist, that which would have been able to exist but did not depend on us. Because we feel ourselves to have been born into a screwed-up age (shall we call it melancholy?) and screwed-up sex (shall we call it homosexuality?) and on and on. The analysis that never surrenders to momentary fashion, its ongoing wrestle with our choices, is what teaches us how to make peace with our regrets. The 'myth of choice', on the other hand, simply makes regret into a pathology: a choice *manqué*. In that case, the better part of poetry or music shrivels to a kind of pathologizing: epic, tragedy, classical literature, the whole lot.

The classical hero is real. He knows that he can change nothing. He carries himself with consistency and dignity. He is weak and majestic at the same time. Additionally he is sincere: he wants to choose, but recognizes that everything has already been decided by forces far greater than his own. The frailty of choice and the grandeur of character is exactly the same thing with him. Hamlet is heroic precisely because he is like Hamlet, and Faust because he is Faustian.

Since we do not choose to have our own thoughts, the same extends our choices. Only rarely do we really choose, the rest of the time we limit ourselves to rationalizing our powerlessness to choose, like the fox before the grapes.

Probably the reason for Lady Diana's enormous popularity is quite simple: for all her frequenting of Hollywood, she represented the opposite kind of human being, the kind for which the public, without being able to say so, has a very great need. She was a type of true human, with whom the public can identify because she embodies the human condition. The kind who does not pretend to have any choice because in fact she does not. The heroic kind because, notwithstanding this incapacity, she continues to act.

To return to Shakespeare: 'We are such stuff as dreams are made on' (*The Tempest* IV.1.156-57). We are not our choices; we are our dreams.

As read to the conference on *The Psychology of Choice* of the Federation of Italian Psychologists, at Conversano (Bari), 1997.

(70) In 'Analysis and tragedy', Chapter 17.